Inculturation

FAITH AND CULTURES SERIES
An Orbis Series on Contextualizing Gospel and Church
General Editor: Robert J. Schreiter, C.PP.S.

The *Faith and Cultures Series* deals with questions that arise as Christian faith attempts to respond to its new global reality. For centuries Christianity and the church were identified with European cultures. Although the roots of Christian tradition lie deep in Semitic cultures and Africa, and although Asian influences on it are well documented, that original diversity was widely forgotten as the church took shape in the West.

Today, as the churches of the Americas, Asia, and Africa take their place alongside older churches of Mediterranean and North Atlantic cultures, they claim the right to express Christian faith in their own idioms, thought patterns, and cultures. To provide a forum for better understanding this process, the Orbis *Faith and Cultures Series* publishes books that illuminate the range of questions that arise from this global challenge.

Orbis and the *Faith and Cultures Series* General Editor invite the submission of manuscripts on relevant topics.

Also in the Series

Faces of Jesus in Africa, Robert J. Schreiter, C.PP.S., Editor
Hispanic Devotional Piety, C. Gilbert Romero
African Theology in Its Social Context, Bénézet Bujo
Models of Contextual Theology, Stephen B. Bevans, S.V.D.
Asian Faces of Jesus, R. S. Sugirtharajah, Editor
Evangelizing the Culture of Modernity, Hervé Carrier, S.J.
St. Martín de Porres: "The Little Stories" and the Semiotics of Culture, Alex García-
   Rivera
The Indian Face of God in Latin America, Manuel M. Marzal, S.J., Eugenio Maurer,
   S.J., Xavierio Albó, S.J., and Bartomeu Melià, S.J.
Towards an African Narrative Theology, Joseph Healey, M.M., and Donald Sybertz,
   M.M.
The New Catholicity: Theology between the Global and the Local, Robert Schreiter,
   C.PP.S
The Earth Is God's: A Theology of American Culture, William A. Dyrness
*Mission and Catechesis: Alexandre de Rhodes and Inculturation in Seventeenth-
   Century Vietnam*, Peter C. Phan
Celebrating Jesus Christ in Africa, François Kabasele Lumbala
Popular Catholicism in a World Church: Seven Case Studies in Inculturation, Tho-
   mas Bamat and Jean-Paul Wiest, Editors

FAITH AND CULTURES SERIES

Inculturation

New Dawn of the Church in Latin America

Diego Irarrázaval

Translated by
Phillip Berryman

ORBIS BOOKS

Maryknoll, New York 10545

The Catholic Foreign Mission Society of America (Maryknoll) recruits and trains people for overseas missionary service. Through Orbis Books, Maryknoll aims to foster the international dialogue that is essential to mission. The books published, however, reflect the opinions of their authors and are not meant to represent the official position of the Society. To obtain more information about Maryknoll and Orbis Books, please visit our website at www.maryknoll.org.

Original Spanish edition, *Inculturación: amancecer eclesial en América Latina*, published by Centro de Estudios y Publicaciones (CEP), Camilo Carrillo 479, Jesús María, Apartado 11-0107, Lima, Peru, copyright © 1998 by Diego Irarrázaval. This book is an abridged and edited version of the original Spanish edition. Chapter 1 on the urgency of inculturation and chapter 7 on educational reform have been omitted from this English translation.

Published by Orbis Books, Maryknoll, New York, U.S.A.

Manufactured in the United States of America.

Manuscript editing and typesetting by Joan Weber Laflamme.

Library of Congress Cataloging-in-Publication Data

Irarrázaval, Diego.
    [Inculturación. English]
    Inculturation : new dawn of the church in Latin America / Diego Irarrázaval ; translated by Phillip Berryman.
       p. cm. — (Faith and cultures series)
    Includes bibliographical references and index.
    ISBN 1-57075-299-0 (pbk.)
    1. Catholic Church—Latin America. 2. Christianity and culture—Latin America. 3. Evangelistic work—Latin America. I. Title. II. Series.

BX1426.2.I7513 2000
282'.8'09051—dc 21

                                        00-028344

Contents

Foreword

Robert J. Schreiter, C.PP.S.

For most readers, the distinctive contribution of Latin American theology to the world church has been the theology of liberation. That theology, powerful in its own location, has in turn influenced similar movements in many other places around the world. Alongside this contribution, another theology has been taking shape in Latin America: a distinctively Latin American theology of inculturation.

Events and environment have shaped what Latin America is now offering us in a theology of inculturation. The long and deep history of popular religion in Latin American Catholicism is today recognized as a rich source of inculturation, as the chapter on the religion of the poor in this volume gladly acknowledges. Liberation theology in its initial phases played down the importance of popular religion as presenting an obstacle to true liberation, but it quickly realized that it was instead a potential resource for life among the poor.

As the author of this volume points out, the 1960s and 1970s found Latin America profoundly caught up in the process of social change. It was a time of both great optimism and acute struggle. The prospect of development promised an alleviation of the grinding poverty that affected most of the population. At the same time, more and more countries came to experience acute political oppression as an ideology of the national security state began to take hold. It was in this crucible that the theology of liberation was born.

By the 1980s the situation was changing. Liberation theologies were under pressure from church authorities, and the structures that supported them were being dismantled. As the globalization of the economy began to take hold, and the military dictatorships started coming to an end, the entire social environment was undergoing profound transformation. Resistance to oppression is one thing; trying to reconstruct a society is quite another. It raises questions of identity that had been submerged in the struggle and in resistance. Identity questions also came to the fore as indigenous peoples of the continent sought recognition in the larger social scene, culminating in 1992 with the celebration of the Year of the Indigenous. One only has to place the CELAM documents of Puebla (1979) alongside those of Santo Domingo (1992) to gauge the extent of change that Latin America has gone through.

Another feature Diego Irarrázaval points to in this book is the reception of modernity in Latin America. He defines modernity as the assertion of rationality, freedom, subjectivity, autonomy, and critical vision. Perhaps more clearly than anywhere else (perhaps because of the great social and economic divide between the rich and middle class on one side, and the many poor on the other), the limits of modernity are much in evidence in Latin America. It is limited in that its promises are fulfilled for the few, and actually create greater inequality and impoverishment for the many. Rather than providing for greater autonomy, it devalues many cultures. Latin Americans live in *tiempos mixtos*—mixed times—in that premodernity, modernity, and postmodernity exist side by side, with many people moving in and out of this complex on a daily basis. As one author has put it, it is the image of a poor man, with his donkey and cart, collecting aluminum cans to take to a recycling center in order to make a little money.

What kind of theology of inculturation does a place like contemporary Latin America, in all its complexity and diversity, produce? It results in a sense of inculturation infused with a profound yearning for life, something it has inherited from the theologies of liberation. It seeks more than recognition; it pursues a quest for liberation in the midst of an affirmation of identity. It wants to recognize the diversity, the paradoxes, and the contradictions that make up contemporary Latin America, and to draw upon the strength of what Irarrázaval calls here its polycentric religiosity to invigorate its life of faith. At the same time, it wants to name the idols that need to be "exculturated," that is, identified for what they are and extirpated from the culture. It also wants to avoid a neo-Christendom model of inculturation that does not respect the contribution of different social sectors of society. And it is suspicious of movements and groups that seek to reestablish ecclesiastical hegemony, and with it, support a form of neocolonialism.

Although Latin American theologies of inculturation may be relative newcomers to a wider audience (this is the first such volume to appear in English), they have something to say to the rest of us. Their experience with the struggles for liberation, their own encounters with modernity, and their long history of popular religion all enrich the larger discussions of inculturation as we enter the twenty-first century. Irarrázaval's work here represents all of this and more. He calls upon a wider discussion in Latin America not known to most outsiders and mediates it to us in a variety of helpful ways. The hope is that readers of this book will find their own thinking on faith and cultures expanded by what he presents here.

Introduction

The yearning of the poor for liberation has stirred Latin American life and thinking since the 1970s. To it has been added work on everyday reality and the religiosity of the people, cultures, youth, ecology, and the gender perspective in the 1980s and 1990s. All these lines of the striving for liberation will serve as guidelines for our journey in the coming years. My intention is to highlight aspects of the journey of inculturation of the people of God in Latin America.

The continent of South America is a mosaic of various kinds of sensitivities, groups, and processes. We belong to modernity with its values and impasses. There are indications that we stand at a change of epoch. It is within this complex and thrilling situation that inculturation takes place. It is not about nostalgia for customs, nor does it mean that the cultural is separated from other aspects of the human condition.

Inculturation is a many-sided and contested matter. Sometimes it is simply a cosmetic makeover to cover huge problems and challenges. Yet in the work I have shared with many people in a number of places in Latin America I have discovered it to be a rich vein of action, thought, and celebration.

In its striving in history the Christian community interacts with the paschal event and evangelizes. That statement may serve as a summary description of inculturation. Thus, it is not an adaptation to each culture nor is it simply a pastoral strategy. Rather, it is a mutual relationship between the human ("cultural") journey of a people on the one hand, and evangelizing action (carried out by the Christian community through its sense of faith, ministries, and charisms) on the other.

The churches of Asia and Africa have taught us to see things from this angle. At a moment of grace, our bishops gathered together in Santo Domingo, and in their conclusions spoke of:

An inculturated evangelization
- That can permeate environments characterized by *urban culture.*
- That can take flesh in *indigenous* and *African American cultures.*
- That has an effective *educational activity* and *modern communications.*

Although this may appear to be something new, living the gospel in an inculturated way has been taking place throughout our history. The existence of a rainbow of Christianities within the multiple population of the people of Latin America indicates the inculturated quality of Christian faith. I call this a "dawn of the church." We revel in the fresh air and warm sun, and we hope for the yet-to-come. The many-cultured countenances of the church are reemerging. In continuing to opt for the life of the poor, the church continues to wager for the new humanity on this earth. All this is the work of the Spirit, who marvelously inspires inculturation.

Yet inculturation is like a weak infant beginning to take its first few steps. It falls down and gets up. Traps lay in wait for it, such as the plan to create a "Christian culture," or perhaps to teach religion on behalf of the modern and postmodern world. Even after the conference of the Latin American and Caribbean church at Santo Domingo, few churches are engaged in the hard work of inculturation.

The sun is dawning, but there are dark clouds and winds that bode ill. Some prefer a monocultural church. However, the forces of the Spirit are moving forward along small trails and through large institutions. The dawn of inculturation is something beautiful, pressing, and deep. This dawn makes the church genuinely catholic. It gives it a new foundation in fidelity to Jesus of Galilee, the only master of inculturation, and to Paul, the evangelizer of Jews, Greeks, and Romans.

In this book I first note the urgency of interaction between gospel and culture. I then move on to discuss the practice of inculturation and its theological foundations. Next, I go into specific fields: inculturations in catechesis, mission, so-called popular religiosity, education, and religious life. I end by suggesting how the Good News puts questions to current worldwide trends commonly called globalization, as well as discuss mistaken and fruitful examples of inculturation in our new global context.

For twenty years I have been privileged to work and live among the Aymara people in Peru. I sincerely thank each person and each faith community with whom I enjoy the new dawn. In the midst of our weaknesses, we are people of God, guided by the Spirit of inculturated love.

This book is the fruit of shared labors. I also hope that the people who patiently read these pages will keep working together in our shared endeavor. A new dawn is occurring in each community, and we feel delightful fresh air in our lungs.

List of Abbreviations

AG	*Ad Gentes (Decree on the Church's Missionary Activity)*, Vatican Council II
Catechesis	Second Latin American Week of Catechesis held in Caracas in 1994
CCC	*Catechism of the Catholic Church* (1992)
DT	Documento de Trabajo of the Fourth General Conference of Bishops, Santo Domingo, 1992
FD	*Fidei Depositum*, John Paul II, 1992
GS	*Gaudium et Spes (Pastoral Constitution on the Church)*, Vatican Council II
LG	*Lumen Gentium (Dogmatic Constitution on the Church)*, Vatican Council II
Medellín	Second General Conference of Bishops, at Medellín
OE	*Orientalium Ecclesiarum (Decree on Eastern Catholic Churches)*, Vatican Council II
PC	*Perfectae Caritatis (Decree on the Appropriate Renewal of the Religious Life)*, Vatican Council II
Puebla	Third General Conference of Bishops, at Puebla
RH	*Redemptor Hominis*, John Paul II, 1979
SC	*Sacrosanctum Concilium (Constitution on the Sacred Liturgy)*, Vatican Council II
SD	Santo Domingo Conference Conclusions
SR	"Secunda Relatio," Santo Domingo, 1982
UR	*Unitatis Redintegratio (Decree on Ecumenism)*, Vatican Council II

1

Practice and Theology

As we begin the twenty-first century and the third millennium, the threads of each culture are interwoven with those of other cultures on a world scale. Cultural autonomy no longer exists, and we now realize that it seldom existed even in earlier centuries; the action of one culture upon another was simply less evident and, in most cases, slower to manifest itself. We are today in a new epoch, and new ways of feeling the obligation to refashion the human condition are emerging. All this means that theology needs to take seriously the process of inculturation. It would be naive and irresponsible to pretend that the evangelization of any particular cultural area can take place without being impinged upon by global influences.

I would suggest that our greatest concern must be the following: how we are to evangelize in a way that points toward the shared attainment of the fullness of life. The aim of evangelization and, therefore, of inculturation is to share the wonderful good news of God's love, not to share a culture, nor is the aim of evangelization one of "evangelizing culture." As we all know, Catholicism first established itself in the Mediterranean basin and later in the entire European landmass. Christianity in other forms also spread eastward, but with the rise of Islam, most of those communities were destroyed or rendered numerically tiny and insignificant on a world historical scale. Practically speaking, then, Catholicism is a product of interaction of Christian faith and European cultures. At a relatively mature period in the development of Catholicism, it was transported into Africa, Asia, and the Americas. In this book we are dealing in particular with the kind of Catholicism that came from Spain and Portugal after 1492, and how it was received and came to be adapted by the peoples of Latin America. That process has been going on now for five hundred years. It did not start yesterday. Mainly what we are dealing with is a peculiarly contemporary understanding and grasp of the process.

During the 1960s and 1970s ideas on social change did not take cultural identities and processes into account. In the 1980s and 1990s we became more alert to our own and other people's identifies and ways of living. This is a major advance. Even so, culture and spirituality tend to be seen in isolation from the press of social and political matters. It is time to adjust and reconsider ways of thinking.

When one travels around various places in Latin America, as I have done, one finds cultural innovations and widespread desires for a better quality of life; one also finds the many-sidedness of the Christian reality. All this is the setting for issues of inculturation.

What is happening in our age? Since the beginning of the twentieth century there are signs that modern civilization has reached an impasse, one that affects it in its entirety and not only some sectors. It seems caught in a trap: it offers human goods without limit, but progress of this kind is not viable. It fails to reach most people, and it is not in harmony with the environment. Modernity spreads one kind of rationality, but a number of other ways of viewing the human condition still persist. We are in the midst of an all-encompassing crisis, although many continue to maintain illusions about unlimited progress.[1] Impoverishment and social anomie are on the rise in Latin America. Those who speak publicly (the political class, religious leaders, judicial bodies, and so forth) are less and less representative. People are ever more indifferent toward structures about which there was agreement until recently. There is a great deal of spiritual unrest. In other words, besides being stuck at a serious impasse, we seem to be moving toward previously unexperienced situations. The indications are that we are entering a new age.

Since Vatican II, church circles have shown greater sensitivity to cultural change. This has been one of the three main coordinates of the bishops' conference at Santo Domingo. It can be a promising vein for the option for the poor. Inculturated churches can open their doors; that is, within the unity of being Catholic there can be a variety of paths, thanks to inculturations made by Latin American and Caribbean communities. By contrast, some sectors of the church are seeking to make everything uniform and propose to redeem modernity through a "Christian culture."[2]

Here I first survey the Latin American scene. Then I review proposals within the church having to do with culture. Next, I note how inculturation is the work of the Spirit and of the people of God as a whole. I conclude by noting some priorities.

LATIN AMERICAN INSURGENCY

Our cultural situation has to do with the everyday, is heterogeneous and conflictive, and involves symbolic processes. All this affects any relevant ecclesial action relating to the realm of culture. Moreover, each culture interacts with others and exists within modern civilization and its crisis. The cultural is not merely "structure" or "meaning of life," because it includes how people suffer, survive, resist, celebrate, work, engage in dialogue, build their differences, and cultivate their identities.

Hence, inculturation takes place in people's day-to-day life, in the unfolding of history. But each human group tends to enclose the Christian experience in constricting frameworks. Hence, along with *in*culturating we must *ex*culturate the message. Each individual tends to absolutize what is his or her own, and the powers-that-be in our Latin American world manipulate the religious factor. How shall we get out of these traps? The experience of God helps overcome the negative elements present in every culture. We question the ethnocentrism that makes us intolerant toward forms differing from our own. In our situation of Latin American modernity, we both inculturate the gospel and exculturate idolatrous human factors.

Another great challenge is the growing and irreversible variety of religious forms produced especially by the poor and the middle classes. This phenomenon of modernity is bringing about a reconceptualization of Catholicism in Latin America.[3] A single behavior—that of poor peoples who love God—embraces several belief systems. These are inculturations made by the people of God, with a greater or lesser degree of Christian symbolism. On this matter opinions vary. If one looks at our situation with a single-culture and single-religion church stance, then such a variety of expressions (which are catalogued as polytheism, superstition, deviation from the truth) is unacceptable. If the stance is one of belief in a God who is savior of all peoples, and from within a church that is multicultural, then there is room for inculturation and for what some call the "in-religionization" of Christianity.[4] In actuality, faith draws together multiple religious mediations.

Yet many aspects are indeed dehumanizing: fundamentalist authoritarianism, polarization around leaders and beliefs, religious division in popular milieux, noninvolvement in social and political matters, and the inability of Christians to understand the emerging urban cultures. In this regard there are renewed efforts at unity around a liberating faith, and here the Catholic church is absolutely necessary.

Religious practice is deepening and diversifying, and yet by contrast church activism is declining. Church renewal, with its range of parish groups and lay movements, continues to move forward, but greater vitality and growth is found in semi-independent groups: popular Catholicism, new syncretisms, and evangelical churches. In addition, a worldly bourgeois impetus "is re-enchanting the world with the magic of the mass media . . . and (with) a rationality that is the new name of divine providence."[5] A kind of religion is exalting modern progress and all-powerful science and technology.

Is this complex scene marked by the spirit of evil that deceives and divides the people of God? Are there signs of the Spirit of life as well? A phenomenological reply is that human beings, through multiple religious practices, express their everyday life and stand in awe at the Mystery. Theologically the "seeds of the Word" and the "charisms of the Spirit" are plain to see; the multiplicity of religious forms in Latin America clearly point to inculturations of Christian faith.

Such cultural insurgency can likewise be observed in *old and new identities*. One great factor is the mobility within and between countries and the hemisphere. Waves of migration in the second half of the twentieth century have drawn a new map of identities. Another great factor is constituted by Latin American ways of living modernity. Hence, in pursuing inculturation, static identities ought not to be assumed, nor should abstract limits like *traditional culture, nation,* and *Latin American ethos.* Rather, what has to be kept in mind is the firm roots that nourish the new configurations; in this regard the changing indigenous, Afro-American, and mestizo features are what stand out.

In other words, the human beings and contexts where inculturation takes place are in flux. The middle classes along with the poor majorities produce a broad spectrum of cultural mixture. The urban multitude has a number of sociocultural models and models of faith, survival practices and traditional faith, desire for integration and renewed faith, search for alternatives, and committed faith.[6] Worldwide progress is skillfully assimilated by indigenous populations within communal and ecological matrices. Afro-American communities are overcoming their internalized denial of blackness and continue to forge their own spaces and symbols. Youth identities are also emerging with generational features, as they choose from elements in the surrounding culture. Women are also rising up with identities of solidarity and alternatives to patriarchal patterns. Each of these groups and sectors, with its own identity, has accepted the gift of Christian faith and has inculturated it, and continues to do so each day.

On what basis then does the community evaluate its own inculturation effort? Some propose that it is the adaptation of the message, translating it and adjusting it to those receiving evangelization. A better criterion is the *interaction* between the gospel and cultures. That is how it is explained in very clear passages at Vatican II (GS 40-44, 58; AG 22), Puebla (400-407), and Santo Domingo: "John Paul II has called [the inculturation process] the 'center, means and aim of the new evangelization.' Authentic Christian values, discerned and assumed in faith, are necessary in order to incarnate the gospel message and the church's reflection and practice into that culture" (229). Why? Because the Risen One and his Spirit are inspiring human history, and they enable the believing community to inculturate the message, and because it is the church community, with its processes and cultural identities, that embodies and understands the message, inculturating it according to the signs of the times in our continent.

In concluding, I note some distinctions. We have already described inculturation. It is different from *acculturation.* In the latter case a person who is evangelizing—with his or her cultural foundation—seeks to fit into and take on the way of being of another people. Something else again is culture-oriented adaptation and pedagogy (catechizing according to the ability of those listening, or a hierarchy that adapts the message to the laity). Inculturation is neither an endeavor from another culture (acultural) nor from a church position (adaptation). Rather, it is the work of each community, challenged by the gospel, the seeds of which are present in every culture, and it obeys the Spirit who transforms history.

DIVERGING TYPES OF ACTIVITY

Our church now by common agreement supports inculturation, although some opt in the direction of a Christian culture. In the past we had a colonizing culture that rejected the way of life of what was native grown; yet we also had the indigenous and mestizo inculturation that took shape in popular religion, the outstanding example being devotion to Our Lady of Guadalupe.[7] We are thus heirs to several ways of being Christian. A broad paradigm has been gaining ground since Vatican II (GS 58), *Evangelii Nuntiandi*, and Puebla: evangelize culture. It embraces the pole of neo-Christendom, a widespread "inculturated pastoral practice," and the pole of inculturating communities. These three practices coexist in the church today, and they became part of what the bishops wrote in Santo Domingo (which confusedly presents all three as inculturation).[8] What is the nature of each?

The traditional and fruitful practice of countless groups and leaders within the church throughout our continent is the *inculturating community*. With its *sensus fidei*, it has accepted the message and produced indigenous, Afro-American, mestizo, and modern urban ways of living the faith, as well as others. We have also drawn encouragement from good work done in Asia and Africa. In Latin America it has been only since the 1980s that inculturation has been spelled out as a pastoral strategy. It is supported by a variety of church forms stimulated by the Spirit of freedom, even in the presence of death.

Inculturation encompasses all aspects of life in faith: ethics and solidarity among persons in need, healing with popular wisdom, faith experience of youth, initiatives by women in grassroots religion, programs of inculturated catechesis, option for the poor in religious life and lay movements, paraliturgies and rituals of the people, and much else besides.

This practice is now enlarging the stream of liberation. Today's base communities are discovering Christ and his reign inculturated. In terms of pastoral reflection,[9] Paulo Suess proposes that inculturation should have a liberating goal and that evangelization should be carried out from within cultures and "historic projects." J. Comblin, F. Damen, L. Boff, P. Trigo, and others among us are dealing with the huge challenges entailed in inculturation.

Inculturation is quite present in Santo Domingo. It is carried out in base communities and particular churches (SR 142, and see 73, 119, 120, 172; DT 509, 514, 677). The final text is clear: inculturation "within each people and community" and through its "integral liberation" (SD 243). The Virgin of Tepeyac is presented by John Paul II (Opening speech at Santo Domingo, 24) as a summation of inculturation. Moreover, evangelization is alert to cultural processes and opts for cultures of the poor (SR 53-56; DT 518-522, 534; SD 248-250). The Holy Spirit is the principle of inculturation (SR 118-120; DT 372; SD 243). All this sketches out a community-oriented and liberating model of the inculturation of the message.

The *neo-Christendom* proposal is a response to secularism. It is different from the colonial framework in which religion organized everything. It seeks to build on three centuries of efforts to set up a "Christian civilization." Now middle- and upper-class groups are trying to redirect human development culturally and spiritually. Its paradigms are (a) incarnation of the Word (each human category would thus be called to define itself as Christian), and (b) a church renewing the unfolding of modernity.

The embodiment of this approach is found in campaigns like Evangelization 2000 and lay movements that are worldwide in nature; both secularization and attaining a "civilization of love" transcend individual nations. This is of concern to movements like Communion and Liberation, Opus Dei, the Neo-catechumenate, Focolari, the Charismatic Renewal, and others. They find support in various places in Rome, but they tend to have trouble in local churches (because they do not fit into joint pastoral planning). It is also the concern of many centers of spirituality and study that develop leaders who combine spirituality and public responsibilities.

Several schools of thought contribute to this practice;[10] they say that they are not part of a new Christendom, but they do propose cultures shaped by religion. In the modernized secular Southern Cone, prominent lay people and clerics (Methol Ferré, G. Carriquiry, L. Gera, P. Bigó), each in his own manner, call for a civilization that would be Christian and oriented toward the masses (that is, without the present schism between elites and people). These people and others who at one point were CELAM advisors (J. Lozano, P. Morandé, J. Terán) are in favor of a people's religiosity that would overcome secularism. Another current emphasizes reconciliation, which is said to be the key to pastoral work and theology; it claims that faith must permeate each culture to make it more human. There is a similar view in the metropolitan areas. As Sebastián observes, "Christian faith is no longer the cultural matrix of Europe"; he calls for "a Europe in which faith and modernity will appear as two reconciled dimensions."[11]

This proposal has entered into church teaching in Latin America as a secondary but persistent line. In Puebla there are brush strokes of neo-Christendom: Catholic substrate and church forging Latin American structures (7, 343, 350, 393, 395, 412, 1099); and Santo Domingo states that every culture becomes Christian through inculturation (13; cf. 24, 27, 31, 33, 45, 97, 229, 263).

Finally, we have an *inculturated pastoral practice*. This is a constant throughout two thousand years of faith. Vatican Council II explains it as a universal plan for which each particular church is responsible (SC 36, 38-40; AG 22; cf. GS 58: image of making each people fruitful out of its own inner self). Included in its beginnings in Latin America have been joint and contextualized pastoral endeavors, the see-judge-celebrate-act method, and a new appreciation of popular religion. In doctrinal terms, inculturated pastoral practice is grounded in Incarnation and Redemption.

Certain noteworthy accomplishments in particular areas can be seen in this pastoral work: education system, social action, human rights, catechesis in each human sphere, and a range of pastoral services (family, the imprisoned, youth, and so forth). Rather than everyone carrying out inculturation, it is done by pastoral agents in these sectors. Besides this limitation, the proposal is not very present in the worlds of the indigenous, blacks, and mestizos.

This type of action is largely that of church bodies. It is more common to speak of evangelizing culture, which would include inculturation.[12] G. Remolina praises the papal manner of presenting it: the gospel is a model that gives shape to culture. J. C. Scannone offers solid contributions: he outlines an entire pastoral approach to culture—modern culture in particular—starting from popular wisdom, and he incorporates the vision of the poor and of liberation; Dom A. Cheuiche speaks of a "double and reciprocal appropriation between gospel and culture"; J. Comblin does a good job of placing inculturation within the history of Latin America; and J. Silva understands inculturation by analogy with Incarnation and views the transformation of culture as an exigency of Redemption.

Church teaching is very illuminating. *Evangelii Nuntiandi* delves deeply into cultural questions (20, 44-45, 48, 63) and even deeper into liberation (29-39). *Redemptoris Missio* defines inculturation as incarnating "the Gospel into different cultures and bringing peoples and cultures into the church community" (52). In Latin America, Puebla is significant for the option for the poor and for pastoral work on culture (385-443). Santo Domingo deepens this vision: inculturation is mentioned particularly with regard to the indigenous and black worlds (SD 243-251) and to urban and modern situations (SD 252, 254, 256, 279).

We therefore have several responses. We now move on to their theological grounding (which is especially supportive of the first proposal, that of the inculturating community).

BIBLICAL AND THEOLOGICAL AUDACITY

We grasp revelation, as it were, in a mirror, through images and concepts that are imperfect but necessary; that is how we know the love of Christ (Eph 3:19) and God who transforms humankind and the universe and who leads us to meet "face to face" (1 Cor 13:9-12). We are accordingly doing a theology of liberating love.

Since inculturation is the church's activity and not a manifestation of God, strictly speaking there is no theology *of* it, but rather there is theology *in* inculturation. The message communicated today is the *what* of inculturation, and the church community is its *who*. That much is clear. What remains is to clarify how it is grounded in Incarnation, Pasch, and Pentecost (*from which* and *how*) and its objective—pastoral method, liberating church, church forging Christian culture (*what for*). This reflection reaffirms the boldness of the Bible, and it is carried out by the believing people whom the Spirit makes the agent of inculturation.

CHRISTIAN ORIGINS

This is how it has been since the *origins of Christianity*. When reread from these concerns the New Testament is full of daring experiences and guidelines. The actions of Jesus and his followers are like a proto-inculturation that defines the subsequent effort. Paul is a very courageous evangelizer and theologian. The Good News is mediated through Judaism and very quickly spreads through other peoples and cultures as well. It is quite astonishing.

The *Son of God* is utterly Jewish and yet also universal. His way of being is centered on the kingdom, which challenges everything (cf. Mk 1:15, Mt 11:4-6, Lk 6:20-26); on love for God and for neighbor—symbolized by a Samaritan (Lk 10:25-37); and on the Passover, whose origins are Jewish but which has an absolutely new meaning (Lk 22:14-20) in the Father-Abba of all (Lk 22:2-4). Jesus teaches in an inculturated way, through prophetic and poetic parables, and through frightening proverbs.[13] His inculturation entails healing sick people (taking on their cries), eating with the excluded (questioning cultural and religious prejudices), and combating evil spirits (who hinder life) (see Mk 1:32-34, 3:10-11, Lk 15:2, Mt 11:19, Lk 4:31ff., 22:20). The Risen Lord who imparts the Spirit has the disciples and the first communities continue an inculturated work "to the ends of the earth," and "to all nations."[14] Hence, the original inculturation comes from the incarnation of the Word, from the ministry of Jesus and his Passover, and from the sending of the Spirit.

Inculturation as such falls to the *communities with their apostles*, by virtue of the impulse of Pentecost. These communities are clearly faithful to their Master—a Jew who interacts with Samaritan people—in their mission in the midst of other cultures. The extremely harsh controversies in Antioch and Jerusalem and the agreements reached (Acts 15, Gal 2) constitute a "first council of inculturation." Catholicity is explicitly combined with the particularity of mission and faith. (This perspective is again taken up at Vatican II, which is also an "inculturating council.")

Why do the communities act this way? Because of the impulse of Pentecost in the Jewish setting (Acts 2:1-24, 2:4, 38, 4:31), in the Gentile setting (Acts 10:44-47, 11:15, 15:8-9), and in the Jewish-Hellenistic setting of the lay church in Antioch (Acts 11:19-21, 13:1-3). The Spirit of Christ impels inculturation forward, but there are also serious conflicts. At the beginning, and over the two-thousand-year journey of the church, the apostles and their successors and believing communities have taken strikingly bold initiatives. The rule has been (and is) "to tell of God's wonders" in every language, in every symbolic universe (Acts 2:11). Inculturation is accordingly not about winning over followers but about giving multicultured witness to the God who saves humankind.

The evangelization and the *thought of John and of Paul* corroborate and deepen what has just been said. Their inculturation of the identity of Christ is remarkable: word, water, bread, light, door, shepherd, resurrection, life, vine; and likewise of prophetic signs of a concrete salvation: water/wine, three cures, bread multiplied, walking on water, raising Lazarus (see Jn 1—12), and "many other signs" (Jn 20:30). As in the synoptics, the Good News is not a storehouse of teaching but an effective symbolic communication.

St. Paul goes further, as he makes a fresh presentation of the gospel in accordance with his Jewish and Gentile interlocutors and identifies with each and every one of them (1 Cor 9:20-23). Paul also argues with the cultural and religious sectarianism of the Judaizers (Rom and Gal) and unabashedly states that the pagan peoples have been saved, and he reformulates the message with elements of their world vision (Eph and Col). At the same time, Paul challenges cultural systems: the weak God is strong—a scandal for Judaism—and the foolish God is wise—something unheard of for Gentiles (1 Cor 1:18-31).

Underlying inculturation is the kenotic mystery of Christ (Phil 2:5-11) and the work of the Spirit. Paul teaches with words learned from the Spirit (1 Cor 2:10-13); the Spirit makes it possible to call God Abba (Gal 4:6, Rom 8:15), as Jesus did, and to live as people arisen (Rom 8:11). The inculturation performed by Paul and his communities is thus paradigmatic.

SYSTEMATIZATION FROM BELOW

From its starting point in these bold origins the church's journey contains a *systematization of inculturation* from below. In Latin America this is carried out by each cultural universe—mestizo, black, indigenous, modern urban, professional middle class, and so forth—and by emerging sectors—youth, women, and base communities. Each informally elaborates its response to the gospel, which includes a theological semiology. The message is grasped semiologically in everyday activity, ritual, ethics, community. (This is distinct from the work of scholars, who cultivate more a hermeneutics of faith than a semiology.)

Within our variety we share some points in common. For example, the soteriology present in the veneration of miraculous images expresses a sense of incarnation as well as a paschal significance. This is the God who is with us, who does not sacralize life but rather transforms and redeems it. The pneumatology of poor communities sustains their own religious leadership, an ethic of reciprocity, and a radical questioning of all dehumanization. Likewise, the people's ecclesiology and sacramentality contains a creative systematization in continuity with that of the New Testament communities, and which is now called the church of the poor. In short, in each category of theological wisdom there is a striking presence of a bold and deeply gospel-inspired inculturation expressing the sociocultural capability of the people of faith.

How, it may be asked, is theology taking up the biblical standard and the unfolding of inculturation by the church in this multifaceted, turbulent situation in Latin America?

The two lines of action already pointed out, inculturated community and inculturated pastoral activity, which often complement one another, have opened the way to *inculturated theologies.* The vast mosaic of base communities entails an ecclesiology—communion in plurality—and contributions to full liberation. Specialized pastoral activities, diocesan programs, lay movements, CLAR (Latin American Conference of Religious), and CELAM (in its Latin American initiatives) also make a contribution. In addition, popular religions have cultivated a remarkably celebratory faith and wisdom. In the ethical experiences of the people and in church action in solidarity, God is understood as life and hope. Bible reading by grassroots groups receives challenges from the incarnate Word. In other words, it is because of the inculturated journey of the church (and not of one expert or another) that we have a kind of thinking that is community oriented, liberating, celebratory, imbued with life and hope, and faithful to the Word.

Because of the range of communities and their differing approaches to God, this deepening is pluralistic. Official teaching gives witness to the faces of Christ (Puebla 31-39, SD 178) by presenting an inculturated Christology. Greater sensitivity to the images of God favors a variety of forms in theology. Yet there are convergences: the living and true God is the meeting point for all such thinking; the same Spirit is the source of different inculturations; and we are called to be a paschal people within particular churches. Thus plurality and unity in the faith are inseparable.

Who are the new actors in church and theology? The same actors who have always been present, but who in recent decades are acting more prominently.[15] Women speak because they sense "God in a different manner," as ineffable mystery, and they speak of Mary and Jesus with religious symbols from popular milieux (Ivone Gebara). Black people see the sacred and God as power and action rather than as object (Guerin Montilius), and so despite the blows they have received, they stand up as a people. Indigenous communities express their vital experience of God with mythical-symbolic language (Eleazar Lopez). In popular (primarily urban and mestizo) cultures and in the religion of the people there is a great deal of resistance and historic power, and that is where the Spirit of God is touched (Pedro Trigo). Ecological experience and perspective "always spoke of God" from Pachamama and Pachayachachic, and also in the Bible and church teaching

(Vladimir Serrano). These very specific new profiles express the human condition as it faces evil and senses the Savior God. Inculturated thought is thus concrete and universal.

These elaborations draw on the achievements of the new theology done in Latin America and the Third World, thanks to the creativity of our peoples and the gospel-inspired and conciliar renewal in the churches. The liberation standpoint is not another set of issues; it is a whole way of doing theology out of the faith and practice of specific communities (instead of applying a uniform body of doctrine to each human group) and of recognizing God on behalf of suffering humankind and its yearning for freedom.

Thus the theoretical framework is not a theology of culture (like that of the developed world) but the thought of the church in our peoples. I briefly note its main suggestive features. The task of evangelizing cultures is inscribed in the unfolding of liberation defined by the God of the poor, and it is different from the proposal for a new Christendom with its notion of the God of providence (Gustavo Gutiérrez). Moreover, we have a theological pluralism: "Each cultural horizon makes possible the discovery of different aspects of the normative experience—the apostolic community—or of the God who becomes present there in faith" (Sergio Silva). Inculturation is a process by which the gospel is assimilated from our cultural matrices, particularly when we move from oppression to life (Leonardo Boff). Moreover, inculturation is already present "in Latin American popular culture, its wisdom, and its religiosity," which is the location from which modern culture should be evangelized (Juan C. Scannone).[16] These are milestones along a journey that has begun, and yet much remains to be discovered.

The point here is not to add some references to culture to scholarly procedures. Nor is it a pastoral concern over contemporary values and anti-values. Rather, we move forward over the terrain of the everyday and its theological challenges. That is where the future of our thinking lies, as P. Trigo and I. Gebara explain.[17]

Over what terrains does inculturated theology advance? In everyday work and drama. That is where the various agents of theology understand the structures of sin and also the creation desired by God, in which we are collaborators. It is also over the terrain of healing, which is a major thrust in the life of the people. Here we understand the power of faith and the saving signs of Christ. Then there is celebration; in the midst of its ambiguities, it enables us to appreciate Pasch and eschatology. The complex Marian cult brings out the feminine side of the sacred, and it is a way of intuiting and pondering the mystery. The community, with its wealth of charisms and its sacramental mission on behalf of humankind, produces an inculturated, liberating, and ecumenical ecclesiology. The ethic of discipleship in accordance with the gift of the kingdom is part of our history and transcends it. There are also other challenges in which everyday events can become theology. In short, everyday experience leads us to think in terms of inculturation.

ACTION OF THE SPIRIT

All of this is ecclesial work, and ultimately it is activity of the Spirit. Inculturation is not some human whim but rather has to do with ongoing inspiration by the Spirit of the Lord. Out of Pentecost, each church and each person continually receives power to witness the wonders of God. The Holy Spirit who "fills" us (Acts 2:4, 4:31, etc.) is like the heart of the inculturation carried out by believers. Far from being a faceless spiritual event, it is the Spirit of the Word Incarnate, of the Easter Christ, of the reign of the "least ones." Hence, to state that inculturation is grounded in Pentecost includes all of salvation history. Yet in all honesty we can see clearly that the Spirit is practically ignored in pastoral work, official teaching, and in theologies. There are exceptions: experiences in base communities, renewal of religious life, and the thought of people like José Comblin and Victor Codina.[18] Latin American theology has emphasized the paschal event and the reign; the Spirit should also be emphasized. Unless all this is taken into account, no genuine inculturation will take place.

This Spirit has opted for the poor, their wisdom and freedom (see Lk 4:18, 10:21, 1 Cor 1:26—2:16); as J. Comblin observes, the Spirit "acts in history through the poor." Those who are "least" in this world and all believers receive the Spirit "so that we may understand the things freely given us by God" (1 Cor 2:12). Insofar as we opt for the wisdom of God who chooses the "least," we come to know the grace of the God of the poor. Inculturation operates in this framework of revelation.

It is also worth recalling that the Spirit is active in creation, in our activity in the world (GS 38-39), throughout human activity ("directs the unfolding of time and renews the face of the earth," GS 26), in the human person with groaning and joy (cf. Rom 8:26, 14:17), and in the contemplation of faith (cf. GS 15). Hence, if the Spirit of God becomes involved in the universe and humankind, inculturation extends to all these dimensions. This is not for the sake of a neo-Christendom or a Christian culture, but rather the Spirit strengthens the "human family [which] strives to make its life more human" (GS 38). Nor is it in intrachurch terms, for that would constrain the Spirit, who indeed calls to the believing community: "Whoever has ears ought to hear what the Spirit says to the churches" (Rv 2:7, 11, 17, 29, 3:6).

Indeed, it is the Spirit who moves us to confess Christ, rock of our faith, and to an endless array of charisms for building up the community (1 Cor 12:3-4, 7, 14:12). This can be seen especially in poor communities, where people are deeply and sincerely attached to Christ, not only through the instruction they receive (which is not much), but through openness to the Spirit. There are many mutual services and charisms of all kinds. One also touches holiness and martyrdom. For my part, I am grateful to the Spirit for the particular persons and communities that thus testify to the Mystery of the Christ, killed and arisen. All this today entails inculturation in Latin American communities. Nevertheless, with the bold original inculturation of Jesus before us, and likewise the work of the first communities of Paul and John, those of us who are now church in this continent of hope are impelled by their audacity.

SAVING AND INCULTURATED SIGNS

The church is sacrament of the salvation of humankind; it is not a body turned in upon itself. It is source of meaning vis-à-vis the impasse of modern civilization, vis-à-vis growing religious pluralism, vis-à-vis old and new identities. The teaching authority of the universal and the local church region demands that cultures be evangelized, and indeed that inculturations be made.[19] Sister churches, especially those in Asia and Africa, encourage us with their experiences and thinking.[20] Developments in Latin America demonstrate a great deal of creativity by inculturating communities in the past and today as well. We see the challenges of inculturation in different contexts, and we are alarmed by trends toward uniformity with eyes closed to the signs of our age.[21]

Matrices and Modernity

Inculturation takes place in certain *primary domains*, namely, the mestizo, Afro-American, and indigenous matrices; their all-encompassing dynamic is urban modernity in Latin America.

Our matrices offer many signs of salvation. Mestizo signs are "popular religiosity . . . an inculturated form of Catholicism," and "faith rooted in the values of the Reign of God" (SD 247, 250; cf. 36, 53). Evangelization inspires mestizo proposals for a new society (including spaces and specific contributions from blacks, indigenous people, and Asians). Such signs among blacks are social resistance, defense of identity, presence of the creator God, and their own religious expressions (SD 246, 249). They also inculturate the message when they struggle for better living conditions, and when they display God's black face. The signs of Amerindians are their human values, world vision, land, organization, presence of the Creator, symbols and rites, theological reflection, and in general, the "inculturation of the Church so as to embody God's reign more fully" (SD 248; see 245, 251). Evangelization seeks neither to marginalize nor to integrate them, but supports their own self-development (SD 251).

Another important domain is urban modernity, which surrounds and transforms the matrices mentioned above. It first requires discernment and then a full range of pastoral planning and programming (SD 252-262). The signs of life that it exhibits are personalization, shared life, openness, diversification, mobility, science, new types of culture, and communication (SD 252-253, 255, 257). This ecclesial task calls for boldness like that of St. Paul, who took a message marked by its rural origins and turned it into languages of faith in urban communities.

All of this offers *fascinating and complex challenges*. The overall challenge is that the message be inculturated and exculturated (as we indicated at the outset) in a modern context that is in crisis, and that the message be embraced as new ways of Latin American life are emerging. The Spirit gives freedom both to appreciate what is good in modernity and to live the faith in building systems that are more human. Another enormous challenge is religious pluralism with its rightful or mistaken strivings for fullness of life. We are beginning to see that the mystery of salvation in Jesus Christ reaches those who practice other religions "through the invisible action of the Spirit."[22] The growth of "independent" churches in Africa and popular evangelism in Latin America (both of them well inculturated) stand in contrast to certain Catholic structures that are inculturated only a little or not at all.

We also witness the emergence of identities, resulting from migration processes, the participation and activism of women, heterogeneous cultural forms of youth, and much more, in the Latin American scene today. Each of these social, ecclesial, and theological developments manifests an inculturation process. They can be brought together in order to contribute from various angles to a liberation project. They can also mutually share their discoveries of the gospel and their images and symbols of the Mystery.

FRUITS AND FLOWERS OF INCULTURATION

We may point to fruits and flowers of inculturation in the realm of church life. In real communities the "seeds of the Word" and of the Spirit who is implicit in them bring about the growth of inculturation with marvelous results. This takes place in all dimensions of being and acting in faith.

Inculturation pertains to the entire people of God; it is not the property of experts or the clergy. Its fruits come from the efforts of the laity in the family, in the church base community, in groups and movements (SD 58, 102), of religious life (SD 87, 91), and of priests and the local church presided over by its bishop (SD 55, 84). The leading role of lay people, which was a major theme in the most recent conference of Latin American bishops, also places them on the front lines of inculturation. Only lay people themselves can spell this out.

Flowers of inculturation are found in the liturgy, sacraments, catechesis, and spirituality (SD 35, 43, 45, 49, 53, 248, 254, 256). Is inculturation growing in each one of these wellsprings of Christian life? For that to take place, slow but bold steps have to be taken. The statement that "through the liturgy the gospel penetrates into the very heart of cultures" (SD 35) has a counterpart: peoples with their cultures reformulate the liturgy and sacramentality (which until now has been kept quite uniform). This happens very little at the official level, but it is widespread within popular religion, its celebrations, and its ethic of solidarity. Likewise, there is more inculturation in "informal" and lay types of catechesis and spirituality. It could be so on all levels. This is how the Spirit works—may the Spirit not be hindered!

The vast area of social and cultural action (politics, human rights, education, mass media, art, etc.) also presents fruits and flowers of inculturation. It is striking that the magisterium generally does not recognize inculturation there, with some exceptions (SD 29, 30, 106, 137, 190, 251). There is a strong tendency to reduce inculturation to religious values, customs, beliefs, and matters. That is not correct, because the Spirit—author of inculturation—is present in nature and the world of today, in history, and in the person.

The most beautiful flower is found when we contemplate God's glory. The Spirit enables us to believe in Jesus Christ and acknowledge God as Abba (1 Cor 12:3, Eph 3:16, Rom 8:15). This can be taken even further: seeing God's glory (Acts 7:55; cf. Jn 1:15, 17:5) in courageous life-witness, in silence, in rejoicing. This is also work of the Spirit and hence forms part of inculturation. We are well aware that contemplating God's glory does not come from spiritual effort—it is sheer gift.

In short, salvific-inculturated signs (in other words, fruits and flowers of inculturation) are cultivated and developed by the church led by the Spirit of the Lord. "Through the Spirit, God's action is continually at work within all cultures" (SD 243). Hence, the particular church "under the action of the Spirit" engages in the "inculturation of the faith" (SD 55). It is not achieved from positions of economic and social power, or with dominant cultural means, or with a church-focused concern. These problems have hindered inculturations in Latin America and the Caribbean. Even so, we find among us practices and ideas that are indeed on the mark.

In concluding, I note two significant developments, one from the past and another from the present.

The Jesuit José de Acosta was a great precursor of inculturation. Even though he lived in the midst of a colonial imposition, he did not allow himself to be swept away by the current but rather gave witness to the action of God and God's Spirit present in the native peoples of this continent. He used to say, "There is no race . . . foreign to gospel salvation, for God does not call anyone without granting that person understanding and grace." He went on to say (surprisingly, at a time when native religions and cultures were being destroyed): God "distributed his spirit and his charisms . . . also to the Gentiles."[23] With clarity and spiritual freedom one can discover, yesterday as well as today, knowledge, grace, salvation, the charisms of the Spirit, present in each people.

A bright contemporary event with long-range implications is the global challenge of inculturation proposed by our bishops gathered in Santo Domingo. We should all have a gospel boldness and should work together in each particular church. Inculturation does not advance through complacency or through individual efforts alone. The task is audacious and it is in church community. As the bishops say, inculturation has as its goal "integral liberation" (SD 243); it is an inculturation "of the church so as to embody God's reign more fully" (SD 248). That does not mean favoring a

"Christian culture" (which in fact would not be feasible). Rather, we ourselves are signs, given the sacramental character of the church, of inculturation-salvation. That is how Jesus acted during his life (see Jn 1— 12). That is how we, his disciples, act, accepting the challenges of contemporary social and cultural processes.

2

Sources

Incarnation, Pasch, and Pentecost

Is the current inculturation of the Christian event also relevant to the two-thirds of humankind whose approaches to transcendence are differ-ent?[1] Is this an arcane concern, or is it a task characteristic of the poor of the world? Is it a sectarian activity in which a "Christianity" stands over against "other cultures"? Or is it rather an ecumenical process? These are urgent questions, because a planetary civilization—with its dehumanizing absolutes—is making its way into local ways of life. These ways of life are being swept toward a "universal civilization" that has a very limited goal: the expansion of Mammon. Even so, signs of an inculturated and liberating faith are found everywhere.

Our church bodies are fearful and ambivalent in this area. We praise inculturation, but then it is de-radicalized and made folkish. It is usually reduced to values and rituals, to tolerant attitudes toward cultures that have long been subjected to discrimination, or to performing some sort of liturgy with novel elements. This must not be how things are done. Inculturation has nothing to do with fragments of reality; it is all embracing and is not circumscribed to the "cultural" or the "religious" in itself. The radical edge is lost when Christianity is regarded as something uniform that needs to be translated into each situation; when, for example, it is claimed that the new catechism is a universal inculturation.[2] In the Latin American and Carib-bean context, the CELAM conference at Santo Domingo presented a proposal that is being silenced and distorted.[3] The infant is not being allowed to walk and talk—but it *has* been born.

My own epistemological option springs out of an Indo-American popula-tion where I live, work, celebrate, and share thinking. It has been inculturating the faith for centuries (there are Quechua, Aymara, mestizo, and other Christianities). Something similar has happened in Afro-American and Asian-American spaces and elsewhere. It seems to me that inculturation is obviously

17

something radical, but far from breaking Christian unity, it is actually a basic condition for making it possible.

In this area the Third World has creatively received Vatican II. From the "evangelization of culture" we have moved to "inculturations." We are re-discovering diversity in unity (see LG 42, 92; UR 4, 16; OE 2); a "living exchange"—not mere adaptation—"is fostered between the Church and the diverse cultures of people" (GS 44; AG 22). We envision the Incarnation, the pascal event, and Pentecost from a type of rationality that is cultivated by people who may be marginalized but are very creative. This is unacceptable in the eyes of those who engage in proselytizing or who "adapt" and "translate" the message. Nor is it pleasing to those who have a uniform and centralizing logic (the powerful) or to fundamentalists, who are widespread among both the educated and the popular masses.

Chapter 1 addressed methodological and theological aspects. The accent in this chapter is on the foundations. Many deal with inculturation primarily as a pastoral tactic to enable people to understand the faith. It is not a tactic; it is an everyday praxis of the people of God and their liberating spirituality. Nor is it something that derives solely from the Incarnation. We must be faithful to the entirety of the Christian event; thus inculturation must be deep, paschal, and pentecostal. Only thus is it relevant for a predominantly non-Christian humankind.

Thus we reaffirm our grounding principles. In doing so we are not excluding other human and religious traditions, nor are our concerns ecclesiastical. One of the criticisms leveled at those who champion inculturation is that they are trying to rebuild a Christian source of power in the midst of modernity and its pluralism. Our concern is not power, but rather the humble foundations established by Jesus of Nazareth and his church. In the present world scene we small Christian communities are signs—not all-powerful machines—of the salvation that the God of Jesus Christ bestows on all humankind.

HUMAN ROUTES TO PLENITUDE

Before considering the sources of inculturated ecclesial action (which is the heart of this chapter), it is well to draw out its relevance for the ways that we exist as human beings. Today, approximately two-thirds of human beings seek and find their personal and spiritual fulfillment without the presence of Christianity. We may therefore ask: How have the basic lines of revelation and salvation intended for every human being become a reality? Are those basic lines an inspiration to non-Christian peoples (unthematically or in some other fashion)? How have they inculturated the communion that we, in our Christian faith, attribute to the incarnate God? We are well aware that each people names what is primary and ultimate in accordance with the path it has taken and according to its symbolism or according to its centuries-old vision. These categories express major human concerns. Are these various experiences and intuitions in dialogue with, or incompatible with, the inculturation of the Christian event?

We are assuming that each person or human association seeks to be fulfilled in terms that are implicitly or explicitly transcendent. The mystery of love is called upon and enjoyed in many ways. It is a journey, marked by stumbling and infidelity, in which the meaning of existence gradually unfolds. Thus we all go along inculturating the search for happiness. Such are the terrains where specifically Christian inculturations sprout, grow, and bear fruit.

We also recognize the many-sided intentionality of moving toward a full life, toward a liberation with all that it entails. That is what is expressed in both the goal and the path followed in innumerable experiences. Yet in many instances positive proposals go hand in hand with dehumanizing means used to bring them about; inconsistency and evil are common. Hence inculturation is inseparable from liberation; the former points to a drive within the complex process summarized by the latter notion.

The current paths of humankind apparently cannot be classified comprehensively. When one recalls the greatest moments and directions that one has had in life and compares them with those of other people, they are not the same. There is no way to make them meet. Even so, there are shared yearnings and practices with regard to what is most significant, with the transcendent. We can say that there are some main routes. Later on we will spell out the grounds of Christian inculturation with regard to those routes.

What we have in mind are supreme routes that intensely embody matters of life and death. They are ways of living that give meaning to death, and ways of facing death that make us value life. Hence we must not limit ourselves to "religious routes," as though they were a sector of existence. Rather, human routes have to do with everything that we enjoy, suffer, and do in common; it is at the heart of all these that there abound religious phenomena around fundamental desires and needs. Nor should there be a list of theistic and non-theistic ways, nor a list of historic forms (where Christianity would be placed) and natural forms (for primitive cultures). Rather, there is an array of paths toward the Mystery, toward that which causes our human condition to tremble, as we touch evil, share beauty, and construct spaces of human progress. This is the sense in which we ask how peoples come close to what is manifested to each of them as the Lovable.

The great human paths may be lined up as follows: harmony in the universe, systems of salvation, absolutes of modernity, fundamentalist structures, and new symbolic configurations. It seems to me that each person adheres with greater or lesser intensity to some basic way of living and dying, and this takes place in groups in particular settings. We are going to take note of these major human orientations in Latin American and Caribbean terms (with some other situations included). We have these orientations in mind when we consider the sources of Christian inculturation.

Cosmic Harmony

Inculturation is relevant for the vast majority of those people of the past and present who seek to survive within a *cosmic harmony and wisdom*. Such human groups are at the far edges of the modern world. They feel the sacred in their entire existence; they interact intensively with their ancestors and with benign and evil spirits; they see woman as a socializing and spiritual center; and they have devised warm rituals and mythical accounts having to do with life and death. Their cosmic and magic orientation has implications for ongoing history; in community they share in events to make them favorable to people who are weak and outcast. When these communities come in contact with foreign Christian missions they intuitively de-Westernize Christianity and root it in a range of local cultures; they enrich it with cosmic values and—at the same time—they open their heart to the newness of Christian salvation. It should be emphasized that this cosmic orientation is cultivated by many people who belong to the great world religions (for example, vast numbers of Catholics have cosmic therapies for achieving health and maintain intense bonds with their ancestors).

These are ways of journeying, living, and dying fashioned by poor communities in city and countryside. They do not call themselves cosmic, but that is what is characteristic about their journey. They have been inculturating their bodily, communal, particular, cosmic faith. In doing so, they implicitly question a modernity that plunders nature and splits persons. How is this an inculturation of the presence and paschal event of Christ and especially of the work of the Spirit? These communities touch the Word, through whom and for whom everything has been created and in whom everything subsists. They also appreciate the pentecostal drive of love in human hearts and a variety of gifts for the common good. Hence peoples who are sometimes called primitive are actually teachers of humankind. Here, the church's inculturating action is not a matter of replacing what is called the natural way of life, but rather rediscovering the holistic and cosmic factor in the Good News. Let us keep in mind that in Galilee the lives of the shepherds, fishermen, diseased, and outcast were marked by natural cycles, ties with their ancestors, "primitive" rituals, and a whole range of beliefs in the sacred. Jesus felt at home with them. That same attitude can characterize the church today. We can take on the cosmic sensitivity of the poor and their inculturating intuitions, and reread our sources under that impulse.

Systems of Salvation

With regard to peoples who have *systems of salvation* (other than Christianity) we are in dialogue and we share with them in accordance with fidelity to the person and activity of Jesus Christ. Our activity is not exclusive or competitive (that is a requirement in the Arab worlds, and in almost all of Asia). Christ is not the property of those of us who bear his name. Is it possible to have dialogue today with Muslims, Hindus, and so forth, as

Jesus did with the Samaritan woman, Nicodemus, and the official at Capharnaum? Do we recognize in the reign those who seem most distant? If the Lord witnessed to by Paul was accepted primarily by the Gentiles, are we giving a similar testimony and do we observe such a welcome among the Gentiles of today?

Those peoples that created major civilizations and religions also have their paths of salvation. They appreciate the transcendence that gives life to everyone in need. Divinity has been made manifest to them. But, as also happens in Christianity, they also have fundamentalist tendencies, whose goal is to conquer the "other" and to set up their own (sectarian) institutions. On the other hand, there are ecumenical tendencies that are faithful to a God of surprise (who cannot be imprisoned either religiously or culturally). It has been well stated that all of us human beings share the question about salvation, although the formulations of the question vary, as do the answers.[4] We can orient that question toward the sources of inculturation to make it relevant for Christian communities and non-Christian communities.

The Muslim journey, within a community striving to be universal, organizes every aspect of life and submits to Allah unconditionally. The Jewish covenant between YHWH and the chosen people entails the salvation of nature and of every living being. Hindu peoples lovingly care for life and venerate sacred signs and divinities who are part of their culture and who sustain human happiness. Buddhism, which is present in so many cultures, tolerates diverse representations of divinity; it is a path for passing through suffering, being compassionate, and bringing about peace. The way (Tao) of Chinese peoples is solid and mysterious, while at the level of ordinary people it includes rituals and beliefs in beings like the Compassionate Kwan-In. These are different systematic ways of feeling, transforming, and transcending reality. These systems are a call (and not an obstacle, as some assume) to inquiring properly about Christian salvation and its inculturation process.

In these settings, the aim is not to facilitate the movement from another religious system into Christianity by leaving behind one's culture of origin. Rather, a Christian practice that is sensitive to the Mystery recognizes the diverse routes over which humankind is saved. These paths are ways of humanization and of engaging with the transcendent. Hence our dialogue with anyone who raises the fundamental question about salvation is a dialogue between believers and recipients of divine grace.

The Christian sources of inculturation do not make it a matter of proselytizing. Without worldly powers (and putting aside many of those that we now bear) we affirm the universality of the Christian event and of the mission to all peoples. We are witnesses to, and worshipers of, the incarnate and paschal God, who is made explicit in unconditional love for neighbor. Those who travel other paths may discover a Christianity that does not nullify their own cultural mediations in cultivating Life. Someone may say that confessing Christ as sole mediator and savior means that "they" are to abandon what they are and become like "us." That does not have to be the case. God speaks to each people and saves it in Jesus Christ, taking on its cultural and spiritual journey. Each people receives the grace of salvation. The characteristic feature of the Christian way is to be disciples and members of the church community guided by the Spirit of Love. With this identity of our own we probe the sources of the inculturation of Christian faith while engaging in dialogue with other systems of salvation that are not devoid of Christ.

Today, as the yearning to do mission *ad gentes* from Latin America to Africa and Asia is growing, we could have a repeat of old kinds of failed communication, or indeed, the conditions could be ripe for a noncolonial spread of the Good News. In this connection contact with communities with Asian roots and others with African heritage, especially in Brazil and the Caribbean, is important.

MODERN ABSOLUTES

In each of our cultural contexts, Christian experience faces *modern absolutes*. When some elements of Christianity are absorbed by these absolutes (for example, free-market Christianity, that is, "Christian liberalism" as understood in the European tradition), exculturation becomes necessary.

Speaking in general terms, a planetary civilization affects ways of life in every people. The problem lies not in modernity as such, but in its impossible promises and its idolatrous aspects. It is not that it is impossible to be Christian within modernity; if we accept that, we decontextualize the faith and deny the freedom of the believer. What is unacceptable is that things that do not grant happiness are deceptively absolutized by that project. People say, "Today it's all about money" or "Science explains everything." These are sacralizations. Yet inculturated faith takes on modern values that help bring about the humanization of all.

What is needed, then, is a discernment of what modernity is about. It does not constitute a religion, nor does it claim to be one, but it includes transcendent features. In addition, today it hinders movement toward greater humanity. Those whose lives are bound up with cosmic ways or who adhere to a system of salvation are tending to absorb modern absolutes: all-powerful science and technology, elite planning, individual autonomy. In response, faith and Christian wisdom seek to assure that the modern is lived as something positive without sacralizing it.

With the eyes of faith we affirm the achievements of modernity: human subjects who transform and acquire knowledge, who enjoy their conveniences, and who organize life. These things can point to Creation and Incarnation. When such achievements are concentrated in a few hands and plunder nature, they have to be challenged and alternatives must be sought. This is part of living the Christian paschal mystery. Every exaggeration of human capacities has to be challenged on the basis of the sources of our faith.

So the Christian event is inculturated not only within each cultural journey but also by critically taking on modernity. Aspects of modernity are thereby de-absolutized so as not to harm the human being. This is done with no nostalgia for the passing of Christendom but rather by searching for viable alternatives. With these concerns we scrutinize the sources of inculturation. Thus we again appreciate the tiny manifestation of the God-with-us. For example, God's manifestation is not about success stories in which some superhuman figures perform secular miracles. And it also challenges modern positivism, to the extent that the latter glosses over suffering and human evil. In this regard the paschal journey from the cross to life is the basis for an inculturation that is alert to everything human. Another challenge is human progress, which modernity makes one-dimensional. This problem is faced with faith in Pentecost, which recognizes capabilities (charisms, in biblical language) within each people in its striving toward fulfillment.

FUNDAMENTALISM

The inculturating process confronts *fundamentalistic structures*, which are all around us today. These one-sided ways of living exclude those who are "different." They are obsessive paths that are based on a human plan (e.g., a model of society), a text treated gnostically (e.g., the Bible), a therapeutic leader, a body of doctrine, an all-absorbing group, or a moral code. Each of these structures offers absolute security.

Each also has certain inculturated features. They are one-sided responses to sets of issues that require comprehensive responses. In a time like our own, when civilizations themselves are in flux, fundamentalistic structures are attractive to those seeking quick solutions. Among Christians, besides vigorous evangelical and syncretist phenomena, Catholic integralism and providentialism are widespread.

They all in some sense draw on and channel unresolved needs that frighten the human soul. Fundamentalism may serve as an (implicit) protest against secularism. It is also an expression of the searching for health by multitudes of the sick and the globally marginalized, as well as searching for community and for consolation in view of today's insecurity.

Yet these are ways of aggressive proselytizing; they exclude other ways of living. They use some things and prohibit others in keeping with thinking based on dichotomies. They make people fanatical, whether about a particular religious direction, or a political plan, or some new aspect of modernity. They reject personal freedom for the sake of discipline and authoritarianism. In some instances they repress everything bodily and celebratory. As a rule they do not assume modern rationality or responsibility for history.

Overcoming such ways of survival requires reaffirming the true foundations. In order to avoid absolutizing either the religious or the mental or the
emotional, it is well to keep present the Incarnation, which situates us within
the full range of the human and the divine. As opposed to the fundamentalist yearning for immediate solutions, we rediscover the paschal and
eschatological sources of inculturation, which make sacrament, witness, and
service to others meaningful. The charisms and manifestations of the Spirit
claimed by many of these experiences should be evaluated with theological
criteria. Life in the Spirit leads not to fanaticism but to openness to all that
is loved by God.

SYMBOLIC CONFIGURATIONS

The *new symbolic configurations* are a stimulus to the inculturation of
the Good News. They are also a wake-up call to our Catholic organizations
and bodies, which often fail to recognize many situations in which human
groups express a reference to the transcendent. There is thus a certain correlation between religious establishments that are disconnected from
contemporary searching, on the one hand, and the multitude of religious
innovations, "spiritual reemergences," and the variety of new symbolic
spaces, on the other.

Such phenomena have many facets—psychosocial, regional, ethnic, economic, emotional, political, mystical. They are not solely religious. The poor
respond primarily to small-scale, effective healing powers and to shrines
frequented by large crowds. Here they find support for their survival needs,
direct contact with the sacred and salvific, as well as identity and social
cohesion. The middle classes cultivate mental power, spiritism, esotericism,
philosophies and religions with Eastern features, ecological practices, theisms,
and humanist currents. These semi-independent movements are widespread
among both Catholics and Protestants and have their own leaderships and
codes. Thus we are witnessing a great deal of diversification and creativity
in the spirituality of Latin American and Caribbean peoples.

Here are some common lines that I find among them. Particularities are
reinforced in response to universal homogenization and as a way for each
human group to hold onto its identity. Another underlying direction is modern religious innovation (the implication is that secularism and atheism affect
only small groups). It often happens that people's whole lives are bound up
with the spiritual movement or group (as happens in fundamentalist structures). Throughout this wide range of phenomena there are distinctively
Christian inculturations, while others bear the stamps of other religions or
indeed are humanistic in orientation. Together they constitute an entire spectrum of challenges for the Catholic community that wishes to be inculturated
in every human endeavor.

Inculturation entails a human dialogue with God. This happens in a
variety of ways in the symbolic currents just mentioned. Some phenomena, however, are centered on themselves and have comprehensive salvific

meaning. They must be questioned from the standpoint of the paschal event. An authentic spirituality deals with suffering in solidarity and strives to bring about worthy conditions for all. In response to expressions that are one-sided (gnostic, charismatic, humanist, etc.) we again raise the issue of faith in the Incarnation and in implications for inculturations. With regard to healing, which is important in a faith that has been inculturated by suffering multitudes, we reread the history of salvation marked by the actions of Jesus and his Spirit, who bring healing.

Let us summarize what has been said thus far. Each group and people journeys toward human and spiritual fullness. These are the contexts for the ecclesial task of inculturation. Such journeys prod us to keep in mind our foundations. We focus primarily on the mysteries of the Incarnation, the paschal event, and Pentecost, because they guide the task of inculturation. Inculturation takes place both in those peoples where there is a Christian institutional presence and in those where such a presence is slight or does not exist. In other words, the sources of inculturation are open to all peoples. In each human journey we recognize the footsteps of the Savior. At the same time these foundations of Christian inculturation make it possible to detect—along each human path—which aspects truly have value and which are dehumanizing.

I repeat something crucial. The sources of inculturation are normative for Christian communities and are relevant for many who have other cosmic and transcendent points of reference. Why? Not because there is some underlying proselytizing agenda. Not because common denominators are invented with a view to erasing different cultures and religions.

How can they be relevant for all? The human condition seeks its fulfillment in a variety of ways. This merges with the dynamic of the sacred, which is always on the side of the human being and every creature and with the primordial truth: the self-manifestation and salvation that the God of Jesus Christ offers to humankind. Indeed, Christian revelation and salvation—sources of inculturation—have to do with all peoples and are offered to them within their journey through history and culture. Hence, the church is not called to impose any Christendom, or neo-Christendom, or any "modern Christian culture." Rather, it is a sacrament, so that each people—with its culture and religion—may find the truth and be transformed by the love of God.

Freedom is a characteristic of the manifold human encounter with the sacred, and above all with the living God. It also characterizes fidelity to the Incarnation, the paschal event, and Pentecost. These mysteries are freely and joyfully experienced and contemplated by each person and by the church community. Here also we see God at work. The saving God freely offers life to all, which means communicating multiculturally and in religious pluralism with humankind. Vatican II stated it emphatically: "The Holy Spirit in a manner known only to God offers to every man the possibility of being associated with this paschal mystery" (GS 22; cf. LG 16; AG 8). This confluence between human journeying and divine grace makes possible, indeed demands, that faith be inculturated.

FOUNDATIONS OF LIBERATING INCULTURATION

METHODOLOGICAL OPTION

Some categories are very much in tune with the grounds of our faith. They express major directions in scripture and church teaching, for example, creation, life, salvation, people. That is not true of *inculturation*—the term is not rooted in the Bible. It comes from contemporary scholarship and has been present in theology and the magisterium only for the past three decades. It does not have a great deal of doctrinal richness except when it is associated with "evangelization of culture." Hence, it is a term whose connection with the sources of faith must be carefully weighed. On the other hand, it is a fresh topic, and so it can be dealt with freely. It is about reading our foundations on the basis of new human identities (poor urban sectors, traditional ethnic groups, women, youth, and so forth) and of the Christian practice of each of these sectors; it is not about a concern for the evangelization of objects of culture.

Another difficulty with this category is that it is often used in a way that is out of tune with reality. It is usually used in connection with practice, where it is diluted and distorted. The fact is that little inculturation takes place as a result of church planning. On the other hand, many initiatives are taken by communities that do not talk about inculturation but are actually doing it. Mestizo, indigenous, and Afro-American types of Christian life are due to the inculturating strength of each believing population, not church leadership.

It is well to be alert to the various church strategies and how they understand the relationship between faith and cultures. We can distinguish the "inculturating community" guided by the Spirit; the proposal for a "Christian culture," meaning inculturation into the project of modernity; and Christ-centered "inculturated pastoral activity" (see chapter 1). These are different tendencies within our church, and it is well to draw their foundations out into the open. The first and the third express greater fidelity to the gospel and to the "signs of the times." The second advocates a way of being church and intends that a new phase of civilization be built upon a Christian foundation.

What are the sources, the saving events that shape inculturation? Incarnation can be understood as "condition," the paschal event as the background of the inculturation "process," and Pentecost as its "driving force." In general terms, the mystery of the death and resurrection of the Son of God is significant when each community inculturates it here and now. It is also significant in dialogue with those who have other transcendent points of references. Hence, the sources have a universal salvific meaning (on the level of faith) and a humanizing meaning (on the anthropological and political levels). Thus they are not paradigms imposed by "us" on "everyone else," but rather something accessible to every human being. It must not be forgotten that inculturation is sustained by each dimension of the saving Mystery: the Trinitarian economy, Creation, the eschaton, the people of God and the church, agape ethics. Here I highlight the Incarnation–paschal event–Pentecost, through which the entire Christian event shines.

Inculturation should not be limited to the analogy with the Incarnation, as is often done. That not only foreshortens inculturating activity, but it also restricts our understanding of God's work and the church's mission. The use of this analogy has led to the notions of the "implanting" and (worse) the "transplanting" of the church from one place to another (rather than growth from within each culture with its seeds of the Word). Moreover, the analogy tends not to take into account conflict in history or the transformation of each culture according to the paradigm of salvation. Our own effort will be to draw out the foundations that are normative in the Catholic community and that are relevant in non-Christian settings.

First, we focus on Latin American and Caribbean communities, for they have been religiously colonized and remain so. This issue is not just another point on the agenda; it is of primary importance. Inculturation is demanded by the foundations of our faith; truly adhering to faith entails doing so in an inculturated and liberating manner. It is also an absolutely necessary task in history. For centuries we have been given a Christianity that was colonizing and (recently) one "adapted" to us. We have been regarded as objects of actions performed by members of "superior" societies. That is why we must decolonize, take on the faith within our cultural journeys, and live with the freedom of the sons and daughters of God. We also ought to stop depending on centers that claim a monopoly over what is religious, exercise our right to be Christians led by the Spirit, and courageously reaffirm our own ways. When we drink from the sources, we no longer go back to drinking artificial and alienating liquids. The local church pursues its journey of inculturation; we leave behind imitation and transplanting of external models, and thus we have our own paths, as the Catholic church truly present in each human journey. At the same time, one can assess complex phenomena, such as the Christian syncretism flourishing in the Americas or the vigorous independent African churches, which have attained (questionable but real) degrees of inculturation.[5]

Second, we discover that the foundations of faith are significant for humanistic (nonreligious) settings and for those who are devoted to other religions. Sectarian theologies are mutually noncommunicative. Our theology does not exclude the other. The Christ of paschal faith is in "the whole world," the Good News is to be preached "to every creature" (Mk 16:15).

It may be said that one finds the Savior God in every culture and every being in the universe. This stands in contrast to a Christo-monism in which the believer stands apart from other saving symbol systems. Within our ranks, Christocentric accents, which are ultimately Christo-monistic, are very much in emphasis. For example, many church representatives are not in communion with the spirituality of the poor, whose religions they erroneously declare not to be Christ-centered. For my part, I see in Catholic pluralism a fruit of the Spirit of the Lord, as is the many-sidedness of religious paths.

The Christian sources of inculturation are no one's private property. They are relevant for all persons who in the midst of uncertainty are seeking, and for those who have saving paths. Although we meet as persons from different religions, we can unite in the option for life. Aloysius Pieris has stated it well: Beyond exclusive or pluralist stances there is room for a "symbiosis of religions," in the sense that we have common legacies and what is specific to each religion.[6] Indeed, the peoples of the earth come together in the struggle against evil, and they adhere to whatever gives life. That being the case, any person finds meaningful a Christian God who is life in abundance. The Logos of creation, the suffering and resurrection of Jesus Christ, and the presence of the Pneuma are inexhaustible wellsprings; they respond to the basic questions of the human condition.

They also speak to the heart of our agonizing peoples who desire compassion; they point toward liberation processes. The horizon of inculturation is not a fragmentary, cultural well-being; nor is it "adapting" Christianity to each person. All the sources of our Christian being point us toward salvation and full liberation. Is that perhaps the goal, and is inculturation, as it were, a path for getting there? Or is it more correct to raise the question of a correlation between them? Or is it better to regard them as adjectives of Christian identity? It seems to me that both point to something radical (and each with what is unique to itself): a sense of liberating inculturation in keeping with the sources of Christianity. Inculturation indicates that thanks to creative, albeit marginalized, identities (typical of the majority of Christian communities) the Christian event is assumed in a variety of ways, and it transforms each culture. Liberation indicates that poor peoples, whom God loves, are moving forward over many paths from inhuman conditions toward conditions of fullness. In other words, these are foundations that show us God in covenant with those who are last, with those who weep, with those who are filled and enjoy happiness (cf. Lk 6:20-26).

This consideration of methodology encourages us not to sacralize the newly minted term *inculturation,* and to move beyond practical pastoral matters to the foundations of the faith. This issue is of value because it points to the demands of the Christian event: to believe as persons with one particular cultural identity or another, to change our lives and our world, and to journey freely toward the reign (cf. Mk 1:15). Let us continue to draw the inculturating demands out of the triptych: the incarnate Word, paschal salvation, the many gifts of Pentecost. This is done in Christian communities and in non-Christian humankind, from which the Word and the Pneuma are never absent.

INCARNATION AS CONDITION

Out of situations of need, aggression, and basic insecurity, one asks: If the life of the people is continually getting worse, how trust in a God-with-us? (Mt 1:23). Likewise, on the basis of experiences of the sacred that enable the poor to go on from one day to the next, one scrutinizes the meaning of the only Son of God Incarnate. Furthermore, a good number of contemporary thinkers look at inculturation by analogy with Incarnation: the direction of the council (AG 10; GS 58) and the pioneering work of theologians like P. Suess, T. Okure, A. Cheuiche, P. Schineller, R. Schreiter, and others.[7] That is, we are approaching this foundational mystery of our faith with the anguish and spirituality of poor peoples and with a contemporary theological sensitivity.

A distinction should be made at the outset. A homogenized, uniformity-seeking "Christianity" is not a source of inculturation, but the Son of God incarnate in Nazareth and forever human in a particular form is such a source. He is eternal and universal as God, as the one sent by the Father; but he is not a being without history. The first foundation for inculturation is thus not "Christianity" but the transcendent Christ present in every human community. How is he present in our soil in the Americas?

For centuries the Christian presence in Latin America was a Christendom tied to colonialism; today it is largely a neo-Christendom absorbed into the project of modernity. But "Christianities" have been of a mestizo, indigenous, black nature and have been from other social and cultural worlds in the Americas as well. In these instances the mystery of the Incarnation is indeed significant, and it opens new horizons. Such Christianities express the scandal of the particularity of Christ, and they set us apart from timeless and spaceless notions of faith. It is certainly true that fidelity to the Incarnation acknowledges God in everything that is human and historic, in flesh, in the cosmos; yet it is also true that we human beings in fact grasp the transcendent through signs in our physical surroundings and in human behavior. It seems to me that this entire embodiment of divinity is a paradox that leads us to contemplation.

It is something marvelous; it seems incredible. The Word of the Triune God assumed human nature in Jesus and ever remains in it. From the standpoint of the Eastern church, we have been divinized; salvation already takes place in Incarnation. According to most popular religions everything speaks of, and everything celebrates, God; we are indeed believers in symbols.

Another paradox is that the one incarnation of God is valid for all humankind. It is a particular event, but it does not exclude; it is a universal revelation that bears the mark of Nazareth, Galilee, and Samaria, and then of every community in the world. In the poor and insignificant Jesus ("Who is this man?" his contemporaries asked) the almighty Father God is made manifest (cf. Mt 11:27, Jn 10:38, 14:9-11, 17:21-22). The practice of the early churches and the journey of the church over the centuries testify that "there is no other name" by which we are to be saved (Acts 4:12). The reflections in Luke and Acts on Jesus and the Spirit, of John on the Logos, and of Paul on kenosis, eschatology, and creation in Christ, agree that in-carnation-salvation affects everything existing and the entirety of human history. In this broad sense Incarnation is "condition" for all inculturation. Hence our inculturating process as Christians does not separate us from each natural, human, or spiritual reality where we happen to be; rather, it drives us to take them on fully.

For specific communities faith in the Incarnation is the basis for new horizons. Of course, one questions practices of the people that are contrary to the presence of the incarnate Word (such as absolutizing something of this modern world or spiritualism). In positive terms, we recognize that "God is a human being and he is so forever; . . . the human being forever articulates the mystery of God," according to K. Rahner's felicitous expression.[8] The upshot is an inculturation that is not sectarian, but rather a being who is fully human and who believes in God incarnate in the midst of the poor. It also means that the primary bearer of inculturation is the poor church community with its cultures and religions.

The paradox of the Incarnation also reminds us of the Mystery present in those who are last (Mt 25:34-45). Today we can say that this means Christ present in blackness, in the mestizo multitude, in women, in indigenous peoples, in youth. Other new horizons are emerging as a result of the holis-tic and cosmic spirituality of women, in the praxis of solidarity that attests to the presence of God-with-us, and in general in those human pointers to Mystery that are assumed by God in becoming incarnate.[9] In short, inculturation is an analogy for the particular incarnation of God that has a universal saving significance. It is the *condition* of the ecclesial task of inculturation. Let us now examine how it works.

PASCHAL EVENT: PROCESS OF INCULTURATION

The believing masses in our continent feel deep compassion toward the Crucified One, and they implicitly feel that the Risen One blesses them. These are two inseparable dimensions of paschal faith; the first has been very much emphasized in evangelization, while only now is the second di-mension beginning to be highlighted. This is the objective event of God, who saves humankind through the death and resurrection of the Lord. In a way, the people live a Christology that springs from soteriology. It is through the experience of being saved from evil and by understanding God's love that most people grasp the paschal event and how it encourages inculturation. This is a process not only because of the greater or lesser degree of conver-sion and human acceptance of the sole Savior, but especially because of the pedagogy of Christ, who walks and shares bread in a redeeming fashion with each people.

The source of inculturation is the living, ecclesial experience of libera-tion in Christ. It is not about "adapting" or "transplanting" what has to do with Christ to a particular group or setting. Our Lord is not distant or removed from our individual or collective journey. Hence, in inculturation the community today discovers and celebrates Christ walking and eating with it, as did the disciples in Emmaus (cf. Lk 24:15). Within each people Jesus Christ takes the initiative and is ever offering his grace and his Spirit (whether or not it is thematically recognized). Vatican II said so clearly: "The Holy Spirit in a manner known only to God offers to every man the possibility of being associated with this paschal mystery" (GS 22; cf. LG 16). Those of us who live this mystery as church cannot downplay or lessen the participation of humankind in the work of the Liberator. In other words, the Christian community can live the Pasch with the cultural and religious categories of each particular setting, as Jesus celebrated the Eucharist in a Jewish setting.

Salvation is given and received in very precise terms: the physical well-being and revindication of those who are outcast (see the replies of Jesus to John's disciples: the blind see . . . [Lk 7:22 ff.]). Inculturation thus takes place through concrete signs in the liberation of the people. If discipleship is a process of assuming the burden of the cross and of finding a new life (cf. Mt 16:24-28, 1 Cor 15:22), then inculturation moves between conditions of hunger and death and conditions of joy and resurrection. Moreover, sal-vation is not attained by following the Law or through power or wisdom. It is received only with faith in the grace of God, who gives us freedom in making us sons and daughters (Rom, Gal, 1 Cor, and 2 Cor).

An inculturation process is thus a journey in faith in which the human activity is not a self-justification but is a response to God's saving initiative. In conclusion, paschal salvation guides inculturation toward a transforma-tion of any situation. This means that inculturation is not focused on culture, but rather points toward full liberation. In the classical expressions it is about salvation from sin (emphasis in the West) and divinization of the human being (accent in the East).

What, then, are the challenges facing communities in the praxis of salva-tion? They must detect Latin American and Caribbean errors in failing to carry out the vocation to be new men and women. Such errors may be classified as anti-paschal: division among the oppressed, aggression against what is mestizo, indigenous, or black; economic exploitation; hedonism; obstacles that hinder the potential of young people and women; dualistic fundamentalisms; and so many more. When such factors include "Chris-tian" legitimations, they must be exculturated from the Christian journey. In other words, things that are contrary to the gospel must be replaced by a genuine inculturation.

In fact, we have many human practices of paschal meaning before our eyes. Even though they are not called such, the truth is that the paschal vocation is internalized and practiced by believers. It is striking how humble people deal with everyday evil and suffering in an inculturated way. Such things tend to be put out of sight by the well educated and powerful (they claim there is no such thing as sin or the devil; they believe problems of suffering can be solved by science and technology). Work and celebration are also very important terrains of paschal experience and hence of the inculturation of faith. Work is very often a kind of collaboration with nature and with other persons in order to move from death (hunger) to life (celebration). The proliferation of celebrations of the people is also (in varying degrees) a process from disintegration toward human fullness and generally includes aspects of transcendence. In Catholic settings, processions, pilgrimages, and religious dancing are paschal metaphors. Another significant fact is how many young people struggle against structures of domestication. In each aspect—dealing with suffering and evil, work, celebration, yearnings of young people—there are signs of the Pasch of Christ; this happens both in those of us who identify ourselves as Christians and in those who have other human and religious orientations. As Vatican II said, all are associated with the paschal mystery.

In short, the liberating Pasch is a source that sustains the inculturation process, encompassing those who are Christians and those who are not. When we inculturate our Christian faith—in each setting and human moment—we offer paschal perspectives on the human condition that are relevant and that touch our own hearts and those of the human beings around us.

PENTECOST: ACTIVE AGENTS OF INCULTURATION

The work of the Spirit constitutes a third and decisive source of inculturation. This is a spiritual drive that ought not to be reduced, as is often the case, to church matters and personal sanctification. Contemporary theology is beginning to see the Spirit in terms of cultures, religions, and liberation. Dom Antonio Cheuiche says that there is a "twofold mutual appropriation" between the gospel and today's cultures, and Archbishop Carrasco points out that the presence of God and Christ precedes evangelization, because "they are the work of the Spirit who breathes where he will."[10] Moreover, we can say that the Spirit of Pentecost gives believers the strength to be "protagonists" of inculturation. Why? Because the power of the Spirit gives us abounding hope (cf. Rom 15:13); it is a power to be witnesses "to the ends of the earth" (Acts 1:8). We have to see what all this implies for the cultures and ways of humanization in today's world.

According to the New Testament, the Spirit is the basis for action. It awakens leadership roles and ministries; at the most important moments of their lives, Jesus and his disciples are clearly led by the Spirit. It guides us to the truth (Jn 16:13). It distributes gifts (especially that of prophecy): "To each is given the manifestation of the Spirit for the common good" (1 Cor 12:7, RSV). Do these gifts remain only within the church? Or is it a power that enables each community to walk with the Lord at the service of the common good? In considering these questions we should review the pentecost process in various social and cultural settings.

Some interpret Pentecost as an isolated event (considering only Acts 2). By studying the texts, we can see in Pentecost various types of participants and various moments. At the outset it is a Jewish-Christian community that receives the courage of the Spirit and speaks in a number of languages (Acts 2:4, 4:31). At other times the key actors are Gentile Christians: a group in the home of Cornelius in Caesarea that also speaks in tongues; a group in Joppa, where the Spirit "fell upon them as it had upon us at the beginning," and on the Gentiles "as on us" (see Acts 10:40-47, 11:15, 15:8-9). In Antioch, the Gentile lay community imposes hands on two people chosen and led by the Spirit and sends them on mission (Acts 13:1-4). That is, various communities—each with its own particular features—receive the Spirit of God and understand the Good News according to their language (cultural world). Moreover, Paul's entire missionary work assumes that faith is not tied to a single symbol system, but that because it is a universal faith it is growing everywhere.

Today, however, we have a very serious problem. The biblical sources and church documents say little about the Spirit being present in the world and in cultures. The accent falls rather on the church and the sanctification of the person. That is how it is presented by Vatican II (LG 12, 15, 22, 27, 39, 44). Only now is a broader vision beginning to emerge: the Spirit is present and affects "society and history, peoples, cultures and religions" (*Redemptoris Missio* 28). This doctrine is necessary for a full inculturation process to take place. Otherwise, only some fragments of the human reality come into contact with the gospel and the result is a superficial correlation between cultures and the Good News.

Our tradition emphasizes that the Holy Spirit sustains the experience of faith ("no one can say 'Jesus is Lord' except by the Holy Spirit" [1 Cor 12:3]) and sustains the universal mission (Acts 1:8). That is, concern for inculturation today is not simply a practical and institutional matter but is something spiritual. We can see that it is a work of the Spirit. Thus, as Paul enumerates certain spiritual fruits (love, joy, peace, perseverance, kindness), today we could add inculturated sensitivity, solidarity with those who are least, community, and so forth. It is my impression that today we see Christian communities, and also humanists and people of other religions, who are full of the courage of the Spirit, with its gifts. The vast potential of Latin American and Caribbean peoples can be attributed to the Spirit.

Yet those factors that we could call anti-Spirit must be unmasked. I have in mind the lack of hope that can stand in the way of changing the current world order, every variety of authoritarian fundamentalism (which also disfigures the Catholic church), lack of dialogue with humanism and with other religions that in their own way have gifts of the Spirit and support the wonderful charisms in the church community. These and other negative factors exist among us in Latin America and elsewhere in the world. Even so, a new

Pentecost is taking place. For example, as M. M'nteba says, inculturation is "assumed existentially in Africa by those who pray the gospel of salvation."[11]

Communities display a wealth of charisms in our continent; the potential is enormous. Works of the Spirit, even though they are generally not called such, are there to be seen: leaders and ministries, loving concern for others, struggle in solidarity on behalf of life, gifts for the common good. Healing stands out. There are countless testimonies of people who feel Christ's salvation in this manner: healing from evil forces, from physical and emotional illnesses, from personal and group frustration, from spiritual uncertainty, from sin. The Spirit-filled presence in the activity of women is also obvious: their orientation to relationship, their work, the way they give life and celebrate it by inculturation. When one carefully observes the behavior and spiritual journeying of people who are not Christian, one admires the deep presence of the Spirit of God (which does not allow itself to be enclosed in one religious tradition or another). In general, it can be said that these things sprout and grow due to the power of the Spirit and to human cooperation with that growth. That is, Pentecost is palpable and real today through many languages, cultures, colors, flavors, melodies, and movements. This pentecostal basis of inculturation makes it dynamic and many-sided. These processes have countless lay leaders; they are not limited to church agents, experts, or hierarchies, but rather involve the people of God with their communities and authorities. Furthermore, they involve human history and the cosmos, churches and the religions of the people, and the twisting path of each human being. It is must be emphasized that God's love and the work of the Spirit know no boundaries.

CONCLUSIONS

The foundations of inculturation are relevant for each human being and each people. Hence, the church's inculturation activity enters into dialogue with those who are not its members. Redemption, as John Paul II has reminded us, is directed at every human being with whom "Christ has been united" (RH 13, 14, 18). This work of the Savior determines the sacramental mission in which the church engages throughout the world.

Exculturation and inculturation have been mentioned. The former has to do with the dehumanization that undermines Christian existence when a culture absorbs and distorts faith. This happens in the ways of life of ordinary people and in the overarching culture of modernity; in each case those dehumanizing elements that attack faith must be exculturated. Genuine inculturation, however, takes place in each particular culture when the Christian community assumes and celebrates the Good News in an inculturated way. With respect to modernity, J. Comblin notes incisively that it does not seem amenable to inculturation, because it is a critique of traditions.[12] Nev-

ertheless, inasmuch as modernity penetrates and reshapes each local culture, it seems to me that inculturation also takes place there, it assessing its
accomplishments and questioning its absolutes.

Another crucial topic is the relationship between liberation and
inculturation; this fruitful relationship characterizes the Latin American
"signs of the times." I believe that it is in keeping with the foundations of
our faith: Trinity, Creation, Incarnation, liberation in Christ, the Spirit in
the world and in the church, and eschatology. The goal of inculturating
activity is the unfolding of salvation. The first theologian in our continent
to work intensively with this topic, Paulo Suess, has put it in these terms:
inculturation precedes and accompanies the advance of liberation, as Incarnation precedes and accompanies the economy of salvation: "The goal of
inculturation is liberation, and the path of liberation is inculturation."[13]
The bishops of the continent-wide meeting in Santo Domingo describe
inculturation as within "each people and community," holding up the goal
of "integral liberation"; they state that its sources are Incarnation, the Pasch,
and Pentecost (SD 243 and 230).

If we realistically evaluate inculturation and its future in our continent
we see several types of action and possibilities. I have highlighted three
strategies. First, the inculturating community; that is the way it has been
carried out for centuries (albeit without using the term *inculturation*).[14] Its
sources are the process of salvation and the work of the Spirit. Another
strategy is to bring about Christian cultures. Sometimes this approach uses
a language of inculturation, but its goal is that the church give a new direction to modernity. John Paul II calls for a "church creating culture in its
relationship with the modern world."[15] The primary proposal is to engage
in an inculturated evangelization; in each setting, the Christian mission takes
on cultural values and confronts dehumanization. This proposal is most
prominent in the church today. But Christian culture must not be confused
with inculturated pastoral activity; what culture brings to the church should
also be emphasized.[16] These last two strategies hold that salvation entails
cultural changes, and they highlight the meaning of the Incarnation. My
position is that unless such strategies are more open to the work of the
Spirit, inculturation does not become a comprehensive transforming process.

A final observation: Reflection on the bases of inculturation springs from
the fact that we all seek to be faithful to the living and loving God.
Inculturation is also significant for contemporary cultures and especially
for the symbol systems of the poor, who are struggling to attain fullness of
life. The foundations of Christian faith are a challenge to each of us and to
each people; they challenge our potentialities and offer us new horizons.

3

Renewal of Catechesis

Our observations spring from concerns, experiences, and questions. How is our catechesis being redirected as a result of the new concern for inculturation? In every region, given its ancestral cultures, as well as those new emerging cultures and modern cultures—that is, given the beautiful rainbow of ways of living—I think it is difficult for evangelization to enter into a good dialogue with those cultures and for true inculturations to be achieved.

Is the Latin American church, which is opting for the poor and for the life of all, opting also for inculturation with its radical implications? What is the connection between one and the other? Can liberation be understood as process and goal, and inculturation as spirituality and methodology?

With regard to the social background of the catechetical renewal, we find several stances. Some wish to respond better to the modern and postmodern. Some are more concerned about the suffering and the wisdom of the broad masses. Certain circles are focused on the doctrinal and moral teaching that must be given to the people. Thus we have differing social and cultural approaches into which strategies for teaching the faith must be placed.

Just what is inculturated catechesis? Is it a new name for more experiential and contextual teaching? How is it different from, and is it in continuity with, what is known as biblical, community, and sacramental catechesis? Can these types also raise the issue of inculturation? The Second Latin American Week of Catechesis held in Caracas in 1994 has shown that today many of us are traveling along the paths of inculturated catechesis.

CULTURES AND INCULTURATIONS

Here the accent falls on the everyday and the heterogeneous. Many people understand *culture* as a uniform whole (they speak of Brazilian, or Latin American, or modern culture). It also tends to be defined with very broad and philosophical categories: relationship with nature, with other persons, and with God. One also often hears it said that a few know a great deal (are more cultured) and that the ordinary people are ignorant. I understand *culture* in terms of the everyday: the meaning of everyday things and happenings, the personal side of things, activities performed, persons, and relationships; culture is lived in all of this. Furthermore, our reality is complex and multidimensional, and the cultural cannot be separated from the social and the religious. Ultimately, what happens in the everyday is like a summation of the human universe.

This is the first clue for our catechetical activity. Taking culture into account means first engaging in a catechesis that is alert to the everyday (and not simply using big abstract words about the cultural). With this starting point, it is no longer a matter of separating a more social evangelization from one that is more cultural; when one is alert to the everyday, all dimensions are interwoven and catechesis can be comprehensive.

What is the everyday in Latin America? Obviously the answer depends on each place and particular moment. Here I will note only some common features.

Our everyday experience is one of being assaulted. All kinds of violence and needs assault our identity (by insisting that what is foreign is better than what is home grown, that male is better than female, that white is above everything else). Millions and millions of malnourished stomachs undergo frightful hunger. Discriminatory structures have been sacralized against what is black, indigenous, or mestizo. Some withstand these everyday experiences with a rebellious spirit in solidarity, but others tend to withdraw into an individualistic and fatalistic world. Self-destruction is also common among the broad masses of the people, as is tripping up one's neighbor who is getting ahead. In our everyday situation we thus run up against an anti-culture of death. Inculturated catechesis is not indifferent to all this; it has to face up to, denounce, and resolve the harsh violence of each day.

Another central feature is simply surviving. With a great deal of weakness and insecurity, people keep going. In large cities the masses survive within so-called informal arrangements (in work, social relations, religious orientation points, and so forth). There are informal approaches for handling illness, resolving conflicts, syncretistic behavior, and the customs of Catholics and Protestants. People also survive informally in families, in organizing self-help groups, in unstable ties of affection, in dependence on protectors and populist leaders. Everyday culture is marked by instability and pressing situations. The inculturation of the teaching of the faith must likewise throb with these everyday needs and fragilities.

Another feature is ritual behavior. The popular masses have endless ceremonies and celebrations of their own; some are personal and family in nature, while others are more social and attract multitudes. Musical and celebratory neo-liturgies of young people are spreading. The market economy includes its own rituals; the huge shopping malls with their ceremonies are fascinating; and consumption involves signs of identity and human status.

All kinds of rituals and myths are being affirmed, right in the midst of secularization. Inculturation is therefore a matter of discerning among the range of rituals and contemporary beliefs, and catechesis has to accentuate its celebratory and symbolic dimension. In broad terms this is a catechesis that is relevant to the everyday, and hence it performs very specific local "mini-inculturations," bearing in mind everyday customs, major and minor types of violence, survival, rituals—in short vis-à-vis each detail of life.

We also find ourselves facing vast cultural processes and a great deal of heterogeneity. Some say that what is proper to us is our mixed-race ancestry, Catholicism, Latin American-ness, or national identity; they say that this is a common substrate and a cultural matrix. I prefer to place the emphasis on the processes that surround us and differentiate us, given the variations in impact according to the conditions in each zone and with each person.

The following processes stand out:

1. A market-based homogenization in cultural products: the culture industry, the mass media, computerization, the worldwide market in consumer goods and their means of advertising. This constitutes, in my view, the weightiest cultural process.[1]

2. Contact between cultures, accented by rapid growth of cities, the impact of the mass media, and migration flows. Some emerging cultures are taking root, particularly in urban spaces, the worlds of youth, and in areas where migration has been greatest.

3. Resistance and cultural creativity by many marginal sectors in a number of directions. There is no single popular culture, even though there are overlaps and mutual contributions within its multiple thrusts.

These processes are assimilated and reformulated in a variety of ways by various human groups in our continent. Although some unifying factors exist, what stands out is the variety of cultural practice. Latin America is like the Amazon River, nourished by many sources and different rivers; water comes in many hues, flows, and speeds. The vast mass of water is heterogeneous, but its various components are in contact and interact with one another.

I briefly note the main flows:

1. Native: there are heavily indigenous areas (Meso-Americans, Quechuas, and others) whose peoples are heirs to pre-Colombian civilizations and who have borne the impact of the colonial age, with varying degrees of mestizaje. There are also hundreds of Amazon cultures, some of which are quite fragile but which are resisting and persisting. The indigenous areas not only constitute our roots, but they guarantee that Latin America can have a positive future in harmony with nature.

2. Afro-Americans: although they suffered from frightful slavery and then agrarian and industrial capitalism, these cultures are very coherent internally and part of the situation surrounding them (made explicit in syncretistic practices). Blackness is more than racial; it is especially cultural and religious. It is contributing to the emerging many-sided Latin American civilization.

3. Peasant streams: this it is a combination of sectors, traditional farmers, modern wage-workers, and day laborers. Their world visions are of enormous value, and their technologies make use of scarce resources for shared benefit.

4. Streams of marginalized city people: these are the most significant and complex cultural fact. These poor and middling sectors give rise to emerging mestizo cultures with contradictory elements: they recreate the popular, assimilate the dominant, and hint at the new. Inculturation in these areas seems to me to be of primary importance.

5. Bearers of the hegemonic culture: the ones who sustain and reproduce the rationality of the individual, technology, and the instrumental market, and the myths spread by the mass media. In each country they are the representatives of a transnational modernity.

This heterogeneous scene, here only outlined, forces us to consider many kinds of inculturation. But all are involved in shared processes, like those that I have noted previously. Hence catechesis, besides being inculturated in each cultural stream in the continent, must also deal with matters of globalization and the ideologies of death that affect us all.

Another huge challenge to evangelization and catechesis is the path of modern civilization. In our circles, there is a debate over whether answers should be provided to the issues raised by modernity, or whether instead the cultural energies of the faith surpass modernity and are an alternative to it. The European debate over the contemporary crisis and modern reason (in which the Frankfurt school stands out) is transferred to our continent. Several approaches have been taken in the area of the social sciences and humanities.[2] One approach is the recovery of what is ours. Rodolfo Kush presents what is distinctive about Western thought: it is causal, asks the why, seeks solutions, exalts the "I am," whereas the thinking of the ordinary people is seminal, asks the how, seeks salvation, and emphasizes a particular condition. Another approach is to retrieve the best of modernity. Aníbal Quijano makes a distinction between the instrumental version and the historic version of modernity. The latter can be combined with Andean rationality; if the private and social is complemented with what is public but not the state, then one can visualize a new world order. Another approach is to question the mythico-economic foundation of the modern. Franz Hinkelammert critiques the world economic system that proclaims an equilibrium and well-being for all that does not really come about; the "total market" is sacralized at the cost of the poor majority in the world. Another approach, that of critical acceptance in which it may be possible to link tradition and modernity, was debated in the catechetical meeting organized by D. Sobrevilla and P. Belaunde.

This debate reappears in discussions in the church and among theologians.[3] Juan Carlos Scannone has systematized the relationship among the wisdom of the people, faith, and theology, the result being a religious and popular way of construing the modern situation. Pedro Morandé detects the split between social models (competition in the market, or classless society) and their ethics, and he questions what operates irrationally and in a dehumanizing way in each model (given the nuclear arms race, dire poverty, environmental destruction, and totalitarianism). Modernization can be accepted, but it must be subordinated to transcendental values; it is also said that our mestizo and Catholic substrate must be the basis for carrying out evangelization. Another angle is that of José Comblin. He assesses the comprehensive vision of culture provided by Vatican II; he notes our cultural history marked by three cycles of conquest (the fifteenth, nineteenth, and twentieth centuries) from which we obtain some benefits; he believes that any culture—black, indigenous, popular, or dominant—needs liberation; he questions the current subordination of the culture to the economic, and our dependence on worldwide North American culture. João B. Libânio draws out the modern illusion—happiness through pleasure, accent on what is individual, and subtle manipulation of freedom—and he notes the challenges to evangelization, which can reaffirm the communal and liberating newness present in the modern.

This useful debate is forcing us to rethink the impact of modernity on Latin America. We have to see to what extent nineteenth-century positivism with its worship of science and technology and twentieth-century developmentalism have been assimilated. While we steer away from the naive belief that human beings are all-powerful and the fanaticism of scientism, we can still reclaim what is positive in the modern and its project of liberation, especially the active cultural and social strivings of the poor. I will go further into this last point.

The wisdom of the people is a fountain of deep and clear waters. In their efforts to survive, people tend to put community and transcendence first. Efforts are made to deal with basic needs by working together; to console one another for shared griefs; to carry out projects that serve the community. Such survival can happen thanks to an intimate and intense contact with transcendent beings: God, the saints, spirits, the dead. The people are impressive in their gratitude, contemplation, and sharing. A joint effort toward humanization thus rests on pillars of community interaction and transcendence.

Another great potentiality is organization. Like tiny ants, the people, small as they are, do things that are marvelous, synchronized, and effective. There are countless grassroots initiatives. Even though women have been kept back, they exercise leadership, bring together liberating energies, and stimulate a "civilization of relationships" (instead of the pseudo-culture of denying the other). The various kinds of communities of faith offer spaces that are alternatives to the discriminating and idolatrous social order. We have here energies, coalitions, political wisdom, and contact with the Mystery.

Another dimension is the utopia and mystique of marginalized peoples. This is a realistic utopia of advancing in solidarity (as opposed to the almost universal tendency toward social climbing and submission). This mystique is essentially celebratory; moreover, people recognize that they are sinners and seek reconciliation. It is a mystique of the future based on the experience of one's forebears. All of this entails a new culture, which trembles with the expectations of those who are "last" and "small," that is, with impossible possibilities.

In conclusion, the road ahead can be understood in several ways. One way is to be concerned with the modern and postmodern, secularization, contemporary spiritual malaise, and accordingly to design a church and a catechesis to bring about a new culture. Another way—where I locate myself—is to take the modern globalized context into account and to emphasize the capabilities and wisdom of the outcast; in church terms one deepens the preferential option for the poor, their cultures, their life projects, their ways of evangelizing.

Let us now move on to the concepts of culture and inculturation. We have described culture in terms of the everyday and the plural; it stands in the tension between globalized and leveling modernity and the wisdoms of the poor and believing people. A basic concept of culture is human action that unveils and gives meaning to reality; it includes subjectivity, thought, faith, symbol systems, norms, behaviors. The word *culture* in European languages comes from Latin, and until the Middle Ages it referred to cultivating a field. With the Enlightenment, nature and culture were said to stand over against one another. The social sciences now offer hundreds of definitions of *culture*.[4] Christian thinking and action need not canonize one or another formula, but it is well to take up functional and comprehensive concepts that enter into dialogue with the theological perspective on the cultural.

Vatican II sees culture in the realms of work, politics, spirituality, and communications: "'culture' . . . indicates all those factors by which man refines and unfolds his manifold spiritual and bodily qualities . . . knowledge and labor . . . renders social life more human . . . improves customs and institutions . . . conserves in his works great spiritual experiences and desires" (GS 53). The bishops at Puebla devoted a great deal of attention to it: "Culture is continually shaped and reshaped by the ongoing life and historical experience of peoples . . . [and] is a historical and social reality. . . . Latin America is made up of different races and cultural groups characterized by varied historical processes. . . . But there are elements that make up what might be called a common cultural patrimony of historical traditions and the Christian faith. . . . [It] embraces the whole life of a people" (Puebla 392, 51, 387; cf. 52-70, 388-389, 409-433).

It is remarkable how quickly the idea of inculturation has become prominent in theology and the teaching of the hierarchy. (In the social sciences, the term refers to assimilating the culture surrounding each person, but it is very little used; it is different from *acculturation*, which refers to change as a result of contact with another culture.) Christian use of the term is recent, namely, in the 1970s in the Philippines, Japan, and elsewhere in Asia.

I would like to adopt two good definitions prepared in India.[5] Theologian M. Dhavamony writes: "Inculturation means the process of infusing the gospel message into the soul of a culture. . . . Christian life is expressed with the elements proper to this culture . . . and the culture itself is evangelized and converted in an enrichment of experience and Christian life"—in other words, a correlation between message and culture. The lay artist Jyoti Sahi writes, "Inculturation is not primarily a matter of converting others but creating a wholeness in oneself. Inculturation is a process of creative expression that enables Christians to be faithful to their particular history and culture within the local church." Thus it is not a pastoral tactic but has to do with being in consonance with one's own culture and history.

The International Theological Commission, in a reflection on this very topic, views it as follows: "The inculturation process can be defined as the effort of the church to make Christ's message penetrate into a specific sociocultural setting, by inviting it to grow according to all its own values, insofar as they can be reconciled with the Gospel."[6]

Thinking on the matter is moving in several directions. The accent is placed on the entire inculturated church, as the message is brought into cultures and the expression of faith is enriched by cultures. There are also biblical, historical, and pastoral studies. Others emphasize the complexity of inculturation, given globalization and in view of the crisis of the cultural as the world undergoes a change of epoch.

My own preference is to insist on the components of inculturation: (1) ecclesial work from the grassroots in which the message is in dialogue with every culture; (2) the Christian truth assumes and questions every culture, and each people creatively comprehends the message of salvation and puts it into practice. It is a many-sided process, given the many-sided presence of the Spirit of God in the peoples and religions of the earth. This inculturation makes a preferential option for the poor and their cultural capabilities, that is to say, both catechizers and catechized are agents of inculturation in community.

Revelation in its biblical witnesses guides us in all inculturating action and spirituality. I pause over these foundations.

BIBLICAL PARADIGMS

Obviously contemporary ideas of culture and inculturation cannot be read back into the biblical texts. We nevertheless approach the message out of our experiences and frameworks. Every effort should be made so that it is the Word that questions and guides thinking.

In the Bible we find many peoples and cultures. It therefore offers us a gold mine for our reflection and action. The entire Bible can be said to be a series of inculturations.

The Old Testament material can be reread from our current concern for inculturation. The relationship between the chosen people and Yahweh goes through several major mediations: the tribal situation of nomadic living, settling down to farming and the city, becoming a nation, living in exile, involvement in wars, establishing alliances, and making peace. Inculturations take place in the realms of prophecy, wisdom, apocalyptic, and messianism. The traditions and institutions of Judaism manifest a many-sided inculturation. I want to emphasize two simultaneous and complementary dynamics. We see first how the Covenant, the Word, and the Spirit permeate everything that happens with the people and transform their way of being. At the same time, the people find their cultural matrices and contacts with other peoples; it is out of them that they enter into dialogue with God, are unfaithful, understand revelation, and write sacred texts. That is, it is God who leads "Old Testament inculturation," and yet it is a human activity with its capabilities and limitations.

With this background we also reread the Incarnation and Christian Passover in an inculturation key.[7] The story of Jesus and the apostolic community offer us the primary paradigms for our inculturating efforts today. But one always remains mindful of the Jewish journey.

Jesus and his followers have an Aramaic and Jewish culture, and they interact with "others," such as the Samaritans. They are faithful to the Law and the prophets. Then the apostolic mission continues in the midst of Judaism and beyond it (Mk 16:15, Mt 28:19). It is a concrete and universal mission. Jesus does not teach like the scribes, nor does he take on a position as a temple official; rather, he questions the dominant cultural order (for example, through proverbs and parables and his contact with sinners and non-Jews). Clearly, Jesus goes beyond Jewish patterns; he gathers a community of disciples, inaugurates a new baptism, issues a call to take up the cross, teaches the beatitudes of the reign and a prayer to Abba, and celebrates his paschal supper. This inculturating innovation is paradigmatic for us.

At Pentecost, the Spirit manifests, among other things, the universality of the Christian presence. It is the Spirit who makes the apostles enter into dialogue with cultures: "All of us hear them speaking in our own tongues of the mighty acts of God" (Acts 2:11). The Pentecost event affirms that divine revelation is without borders: the Word and the Spirit are given to all peoples. This is the founding event of the inculturation that the church has to carry out.

These are models that inspire inculturated catechesis today. I pause over several aspects, which have already been developed by Paulo Suess.[8]

FAITH AND CULTURAL FURROW

The early Christians had differences, discrimination, and conflicts with their cultural aspects (if such modern terminology can be used). We are struck by the sharp tension between Hebrews and Hellenists. The dispute

had already existed for a long time. In Judaism before Jesus some spoke
Aramaic and others in the diaspora used Greek; they had the same Law, but
they met in different synagogues. This is helpful for understanding the con-
frontation during the apostolic age. It occurs despite the behavior of Jesus
and the command at Pentecost. There at the beginning of the church, as
throughout its history, inculturation is a process involving conflict. The
paradigm for us is to resolve conflict so that faith in Christ can develop with
its newness and transcendence.

The Hebrews had the twelve apostles; the Hellenists complained and
chose seven servants who were commissioned by imposition of hands (Acts
6:1-6). In addition, because of persecution by Jewish authorities, the believers had to go out and live among other cultures, without ties to the temple
or the Law; in Antioch (Syria) they were called Christians (Acts 11:26).

A series of incidents and clashes between Jewish Christians and Gentile
Christians takes place. They do not become part of various cultures in a
peaceful and quick process. A major step in this process takes place at the
so-called Council of Jerusalem (A.D. 48-49) with its decisive cultural and
religious repercussions. The Hellenists are not burdened with Jewish re-
quirements (such as circumcision), except for not eating meat offered to
idols and not having illegitimate unions (Acts 15:5-9, Gal 2:1-10). It seems
that difficulties continued on an everyday level. Paul and Peter argue over
whether a Jew could eat with Gentiles (Gal 2:11-21). Inculturation has always been hotly polemical.

Thus the same faith continues to grow along different furrows. The
struggle is long and difficult. Ultimately, the Christian faith and the communication of the message are carried out in several ways. It is not a
single-culture or ethnocentric work. In the midst of clashes, the Spirit guides
the infant church: "The Holy Spirit and we have decided" (Acts 15:28).
Each human culture is able to receive faith and can respond to the Message
and the movement of the Spirit. This is our paradigm for catechesis: our
common faith moves forward like water through different irrigation ditches
and gives new life to all cultures.

PAUL'S MISSION

Faithful to the nondiscriminatory spirit of Jesus, Paul's work of evangelization is paradigmatic. The believers continue with their customs, but they
also get some distance from them so as to relish a new life in Christ. Paul
himself embodies various kinds of inculturation, as a Jew and Pharisee, as a
Roman citizen and one located in pagan settings. He can be called the first
catechist of inculturation (in the apostolic church), and we can regard Stephen
as the first martyr of inculturation.

How does Paul teach the faith? First, he stands in continuity with what
has been lived in each culture. The evangelizer becomes Jewish with the
Jews and behaves as a Gentile with non-Jews ("I have become all things to

all" [1 Cor 9:20-23]). The evangelized community must not be exculturated or alienated; the Gentile does not have to be Judaized, and the circumcised do not have to be de-Judaized. This stance even brings Paul to admire people in an idolatrous world; he admires the religion to the unknown God in Athens ("What you unknowingly worship, I proclaim to you" [Acts 17:22-28]). That is, conversion to the Risen Lord does not nullify the cultural situation of believers. That is where they practice their new faith.

Second, there is a break. Basically, this means that the person who is a disciple must shun evil. Jews and Gentiles have been immersed in sin and they are only justified by faith (Rom 1:16—3:31). They are not saved by "works" according to the Law of the Jew or by the "wisdom" of the Greek. That is, their cultures, their human and religious efforts, are surpassed by the faith that responds to the redeeming message. The works of the Law have no value in themselves, for the Law brings a curse and its only value is as pedagogy toward Christ (Gal 3:10-24). Faith does not come from human wisdom; it is the Spirit who makes divine grace known (1 Cor 1:17-2:16). These breaks do not make believers abandon the culture of Jerusalem, Corinth, and so forth. Each new disciple remains in his or her social and cultural space but is baptized there and brought into a new community, and in that sense there is a break.

It is paradoxical: One remains in the culture and yet must withdraw from the evil in it; one shares work and feelings with one's neighbor, and yet sees that salvation comes not from shared customs but from the liberating God. This is demanded by the new life in Christ. It seems to me that the Pauline paradigm means two things for us. The believing community fully reaffirms its social and cultural identity and on that basis agrees to be a disciple of the Lord Jesus. At the same time the believing community de-absolutizes its human and cultural setting; it breaks with those things that are filled with sin; it is converted; and it enjoys the freedom granted by the Spirit of the Lord.

GOSPEL OF THE IGNORANT BUT WISE

Dominant thinking is different from the wisdom of the people who seem to be insignificant. This is another New Testament paradigm. The liberating message challenges the former and shows preference for the latter.

Jesus engages in dialogue with various persons and groups, with the cultural levels of his age. But his main interlocutors are those classified as ignorant and sinful: marginal people, children, women, lepers, and the sick. These are the people closest to Jesus: he speaks with them, listens to them, walks with them, heals them, calls them blessed.

This stands in contrast with customs that were then very deep-seated. Jewish society was very discriminatory in both religion and culture. A little boy or girl was said not to know anything. Women were kept away from education and power. The whole multitude of the poor, the sick, and sinners was viewed with contempt by people who were "cultured" and observed the Law.

Yet these are the people with whom Jesus spends his time, becomes friends, welcomes, and teaches (see Lk 7:22, 8:1-3, 9:48, 10:21, 39, 14:23-24, 18:15-17). Jesus can be said to opt culturally for people who are supposedly ignorant. He shows affection for them. He takes on their needs and ways of understanding everyday matters. He shares their yearnings and feelings. He enters into their environment of marginal culture and into their ways of showing solidarity. Given this fundamental stance, it is not surprising that Jesus is continually in conflict with those who regard themselves as possessors of the truth and upholders of morality (Mt 5:20 ff., 15:1-9, 23:1-32). Jesus is certain that God makes the humble wise (Mt 25). Those cast out by the dominant culture are the ones who best know God.

St. Paul continues with this perspective, which overturns the social and cultural order. The people and communities regarded as stupid, powerless, and ignorant are the Lord's favorites. According to Paul, God surprisingly chooses what is foolish and weak (1 Cor 1:26-29). That's why they should become foolish in order to be wise (1 Cor 3:18-20). The only source of truth is God. Elsewhere, Paul criticizes a "truth" that is in league with injustice (Rom 1:18, Col 2:8) and the thinking of those who rule in the world (1 Cor 2:6). The letter of James also distinguishes a true wisdom from that which is false (Jas 3:13-18), using as a criterion behavior toward one's neighbor, of "deeds done in the gentleness of wisdom."

If we check this paradigm against the Latin American situation, the teaching of the faith is aimed at the multitude whom those above call superstitious and ignorant. But it is they who are full of the wisdom that God grants to the least. In other words, inculturated catechesis stands apart from dominant thinking and is in tune with marginal ways of life.

The biblical paradigm thus urges the inculturation of contemporary catechesis. This takes place thanks to the Spirit. It is not a tactic. The task is not to adapt the message and adjust it to a human context; rather, it is the Spirit who leads the faithful people to the fullness of truth. I have noted some biblical paradigms: faith running like water through various furrows of culture; continuity with, and break from, the things that condition us socially and culturally (St. Paul); and preference for the wisdom of the least. By taking inspiration from these and other biblical paradigms, catechesis is renewed and inculturated. This is effective insofar as it is the fruit of the Spirit who guides the church.

What we call inculturation today has been present throughout church history. Thus it can be found in the Fathers (and Mothers) of the church, the witness of martyrs and saints, the many-sided unfolding of the liturgy, and especially the sacramentals, iconography with features from many worlds, the local and universal magisterium, the currents of popular religion, and much more. (The persistence of the inculturations achieved in medieval Europe and periodically restored in subsequent centuries is striking.) The Christian life has been incarnated in many historical forms; it is a sign of how the Spirit has moved and continues to drive the people of God. One sees that failure to inculturate catechesis seems to entail infidelity to the Spirit.

GUIDELINES FROM CHURCH TEACHING

We start with Vatican II and will then also take into account Latin American teaching and practice.

CONCILIAR RENEWAL

The idea of inculturation was not used in the 1960s, but Vatican Council II (1962-65) provides doctrinal support for it; we find the cultural at the very heart of the conciliar teaching.

On the relationship between revelation and cultures: "For God, revealing himself to his people to the extent of a full manifestation of himself in his Incarnate Son, has spoken according to the culture proper to different ages" (GS 58). With regard to the Incarnation and cultures: "In order to offer to all . . . the mystery of salvation and the life brought by God, the Church must become part of all these groups for the same motive which led Christ to bind Himself, in virtue of His Incarnation, to the definite social and cultural conditions of those human beings among whom He dwelt" (AG 10). In other words, that is how God acts (self-revelation, incarnation in cultures), and that is how the church teaches out of different cultures and located within them. This teaching is destined to provide the basis for gradually moving away from the traditional stance of adaptation and accommodation to one of contextualization and inculturation.[9]

The treatment given to the cultural in *Gaudium et Spes* (53-62) should also be taken into account. Stress is placed on scientific progress and Western technology, and the tensions that emerge there. It is also noteworthy that culture is understood to mean not values or the heritage of cultivated groups but as part of the unfolding of events now and as shared possession. Another great truth is that church and cultures (GS 58; cf. 40-44) and church and world enrich one another; this viewpoint is different from that of an "adaptation" of Christian life to each culture (AG 22; GS 91). It is striking that these conciliar texts combine different approaches to culture (as often happens in official texts). In short, the reception of Vatican II has made possible a more effective evangelization of the cultural depth of each people. Let us look at what has happened in Latin America.

BISHOPS IN MEDELLÍN, PUEBLA, AND SANTO DOMINGO

At their 1968 meeting in Medellín the bishops considered the change taking place in Latin America and the presence of the church in this process.

That is the standpoint from which catechesis and its renewal are viewed. The "signs of the times" present the need for a deep renewal (Medellín Catechesis 1, 2, 3, 5): because the world changes, the church matures, and popular religion remains. The theological perspective there shows the unity between God's design and human aspirations (6); hence the history of humankind is part of the content of catechesis. When real life is related to the message, there must be "fidelity to the revealed Word" (15). Even though the word *inculturation* is not used, that is the meaning of these texts.

With regard to methodology, the diversity of situations and cultures requires that there be multiple forms of catechesis (8, 15). Emphasis is placed on the aspects of community and family in catechesis (10), the new culture of the image (12), and the training of lay catechists in all locations (14, 17). Both doctrinal foundations and guidelines for activity are intended to change catechesis (as it opens up to inculturation).

The central question at Puebla (1979) was evangelization, and evangelizing culture in particular. The Christian message must be transmitted in its entirety (Puebla 1004). Advances are made in fields related to what we are discussing here: evangelization and culture (385-443), popular religiosity (444-469), liberation (470-506), and catechesis (977-1011). What is called for is a catechesis that will "penetrate, take up, and purify the values of their culture" (996). With regard to methodologies the bishops speak of catechesis of groups or multitudes (1010), and the use of human memory and audiovisual techniques (1009). Emphasis is placed on the complex process of contemporary culture (393, 421-443). The dawning universal culture is critiqued for its "uniformity and leveling, that fails to respect different cultures" (427). The birth of a new civilization of communion and participation, a new humankind, is regarded as positive (350). Many people have been sensitized by these guidelines; thanks to Puebla, catechesis has become more concerned with the culture. But the issue of inculturation has yet to be faced.

In 1992 the bishops of the continent restated at Santo Domingo the issues of evangelization in connection with human development and culture. As had been the case at Puebla, Santo Domingo did not go deeply into catechesis; but everything said about inculturation is certainly relevant. Catechesis is defined as ongoing education of faith, and is spoken of in terms of revelation and discipleship; it is celebrated in community and is Good News for our times and situation (see SD 33, 49, 142, 239, 302). The problems are presented religious ignorance, superficial forms, incomplete contents, and failure to transform life and environments (41). With regard to who does catechesis, lay people are praised (19, 41, 101) and Afro-American catechists are mentioned (19). No connection is drawn between inculturation and catechesis (except for 49 and 189: catechists inculturate the gospel); even so, one can apply Santo Domingo's excellent message on inculturation to the specific field of catechesis.

PAUL VI AND JOHN PAUL II

As a follow-up to the Synod on Evangelization, Paul VI issued *Evangelii Nuntiandi* (1975), which takes up the drama of our time: the split between the gospel and culture. Hence cultures must be evangelized "in depth and right to their very roots" (20). Another noteworthy point is linking the reign with culture: "The building up of the Kingdom cannot avoid borrowing the elements of human culture or cultures" (20). Catechesis is understood as "systematic religious instruction [in] the fundamental teachings" with methods "adapted to the age, culture, and aptitude of . . . persons" (44; cf. 54). There is talk of "adaptation" (44, 54) and yet also of impregnation, regeneration, and "unceasing interplay of the Gospel and of man's concrete life, both personal and social" (29, see also 20). Interaction and dialogue give inculturation its shape, I believe, and this does not happen when what is called for is adaptation and mere translation of the message.

John Paul II has new things to say about inculturated catechesis. In *Catechesi Tradendae* (1979) the pope presents conclusions of a synod on the issue. The doctrinal foundations are Christ as sole Master (6-9), the church's mission (10-17, 62-71), and the work of the Spirit (72). Catechesis is defined as a moment in the evangelization process; it cultivates the faith of children, young people, and adults, teaching them "Christian doctrine . . . in an organic and systematic way" (18). John Paul II points to a variety and complementarity of programs, in accordance with those to whom they are addressed and the social and cultural milieux in which they unfold (45, 51). The central point is that catechesis is to be incarnated in cultures, while avoiding any kind of reductionism or concessions in issues of faith and morality (53).

The pope speaks here about inculturation as a component of Incarnation. He makes two important points: the gospel is always set within cultures, and the "power of the Gospel . . . transforms and renews" cultures. He also speaks of the religion and culture of the people, which are helpful for better understanding the Christian mystery (53). In another document, *Slavorum Apostoli* (1985), John Paul II speaks a great deal about inculturation, as "incarnation of the Gospel in native cultures bring[s] them into the life of the church" (21; cf. 26). Thus we have a twofold movement: from the gospel and the mission of the church to cultures, and from peoples and cultures to the message. This interaction is the core of inculturation in all evangelization, particularly in catechesis.

CATECHISM OF THE CATHOLIC CHURCH

This monumental work, which was completed and published in 1992, is a valuable "reference text," as the pope says in *Fidei Depositum* (1, 4). It is not supposed to replace local catechisms, but rather encourage their preparation, in view of "different situations and cultures" (FD 4); the catechism of each place and those who instruct the faithful are to make "adaptations" (Prologue, 24). The underlying issue is the "pedagogy of God's saving love" (CCC 122). This can be done within an approach based on concepts and adaptation or one that is mystagogical and inculturated.

The new catechism does not say much about cultures. It notes the diversity of cultures and says that the unity of the church and of the people of God contains different types of persons, peoples, and cultures (814). This diversity implies the existence of different types of catechisms (24), different expressions of catholicity (835), and complementarity between cultures (1937). Inculturating activity is also mentioned. With a reference to *Redemptoris Missio*, the catechism speaks of the "inculturation process so as to incarnate the Gospel in the cultures of peoples" (854). "Through many languages, cultures . . . the church unceasingly confesses its one faith" (172). Because it is Catholic, the liturgy incorporates elements from cultures (cf. 1149, 1202).

Clear thinking and caution are called for in this area. A distinction, but not a separation, must be made between "growth of the Reign of God and the progress of culture and development of society" and the calling to eternal life that entails working for justice and peace in this world (2820). In my understanding, God is manifest to humankind in such a way that the church's mission—and specifically the task of catechesis—is to give witness to love in educating faith in an ongoing way. This mission is incomplete if all that happens is a conceptual adaptation of the message to each setting. In my view, a mystagogical catechesis that entails inculturation is more faithful to revelation, to the mystery of the growth of the reign, and to the presence of the Spirit.[10]

In summary, I would say that today's talk of inculturation is not simply a repeat of what used to be said; a further step has been taken. The implications of the Incarnation and of the world of the Spirit are being rediscovered, in the sense of a catechesis that brings the life of the people of God into interaction with the saving message. This interaction is different from mere adaptation. This is a new horizon both conceptually and in practice.

PROGRAMMATIC ADVANCES

It is clear that in fidelity to the message and embodying the guidelines provided for the teaching and life of the church, recent years have been rich in catechetical experiences and programs. Steps toward deep renewal are being taken, but inculturation is still incipient and timid. Let us look at some general proposals (as expressed by CELAM bodies and events) and then at plans carried out in several Latin American countries.

CELAM INITIATIVES

The great extent and complexity of Latin America require specific catechesis and also common guidelines. CELAM is among those making contributions along these lines. I will examine here a 1986 document and an event on inculturation in 1994.[11]

The 1986 guidelines draw on a vast torrent of experiences and thinking from the entire continent. Catechesis is described with a beautiful image of journey: "ongoing journey toward the fullness of the Revelation made by God in becoming human in Jesus" (48). The guidelines emphasize that catechesis is community based, situational, missionary, and liberating. Catechesis "assumes and purifies" cultures and there is a "close relationship between the formulation of the divine message and the various cultures" (149 and 146).

Issues of inculturation are treated from three angles. First comes the great principle of the interaction between message and life (21-22). It is not a matter of applying and injecting doctrine. Rather, teaching the faith is a process of mutual questioning between the Word and the human condition. Second, the CELAM texts present the inculturating mode quite plainly: "One aspect of catechesis can never be neglected: listening, seeing, and sharing the life of the people. . . . In listening to God's action present in society, in distinguishing the signs of the times . . . the one faith is being incarnated in new cultural worlds" (230). The third aspect is the close connection between catechesis and popular religion. It is a service to religiosity, forming faith out of religiosity, inasmuch as this religiosity is like an inexhaustible quarry of subject matter for educating faith (105-120).

Thus a "map" has been drawn for pastoral activity. It shows where we are going and how to move forward, and so I call it a map.

This advance has been ratified by the Second Latin American Week organized by CELAM (1994) and has received feedback there. The conclusions of the week provide a thorough explanation of inculturated catechesis: Christ is the center, the history of this type of catechesis, its theological foundations and proposals for action. It is repeatedly presented as a process (18, 32, 43, 80, 82, 96, 107, 116) in native cultures as well as in modernity and postmodernity (28). A great deal of importance is given to the principles of inculturation used by Jesus (57-68). At the same time, culture must not be overvalued (cf. 96); catechesis inculturates Christ in all settings and emphasizes solidarity and social justice (42).

The people's religion is treated as a privileged location for inculturated catechesis (83; cf. 25, 120, 144, 167, 182). I am going to pause over this point. It is widely known that the people's religion has its positive and negative features; the point is to bring it to maturity in its gospel and ecclesial content from within (and not with attitudes of a supposedly superior and pure culture and faith)—that is, to begin from the experience of God that Latin American people already have, including the way that experience is mediated. A basic issue here is celebratory catechesis; in this regard it is said that there should be support for "popular religious celebrations so that even those whose origins are not Christian can constitute or support a great popular catechesis, using all the signs, values and languages compatible with the

Gospel to touch the heart of cultures" (182). I am convinced that the most important aspect of inculturated catechesis is the symbolic (rather than the conceptual).

BRAZIL AND ECUADOR: SOCIETY AND CULTURES

It is not easy to interweave the social and the cultural. In this regard the doctrinal guidelines of the Brazilian bishops and some materials from Ecuador are instructive.[12]

The theoretical framework of *Catechese Renovada,* which is the product of a rich Brazilian ecclesial experience, has two significant terms: *journey* and *community.* This is a community process of holistic education of the faith, where the acting subject is the community (281-317). There is a social accent, not in the restricted sense of social phenomena but in the entire human condition that receives revelation. God is made manifest in history, catechesis is carried out by a specific community, and the option is for full liberation. Thus inculturation will not be carried out episodically and as folklore, and full teaching of the faith has implications for personal and social transformation.

In terms of methodology catechesis follows the principle of interaction— mutual and effective relationship between the experience of life and the formulation of the faith (113). This clear principle of interaction is what will later be called inculturation. The Brazilian document indeed mentions "adaptation" in language, method, and content, in view of the historic and cultural conditions of those being catechized (101). As I have already pointed out, these are two different lines; the first is deep and comprehensive and better displays the process of faith.

The Ecuadorian "En route toward the Reign of God" is among many efforts at inculturated and liberating catechesis. It is not a catechism but working materials in the form of a series of themes: family, youth, work, basic needs, rich and poor, culture, dependence, religiosity, community and organization, ministries, and so forth. Each theme has four dimensions: God's plan, our situation, life in Christ, church and reign. Interaction between faith and life is obvious.

By way of example, I take the worksheet that deals with culture. It has a biblical starting point: God manifests Godself in the culture of each people; idolatry is distinguished from faith in the one God; the unity of humankind is confirmed. Then there is mention of the various cultures in Ecuador: domination, education, positive and negative features. The central part is Christological: Jesus takes on the identity of his people, Jesus helps change and humanize culture. There are examples of the church inculturated and observations on the building of the kingdom in Ecuadorian settings.

These two contributions develop the sociocultural dimensions of catechesis; what makes this possible is the fruitful method and spirit of interaction between the message and the daily life of the people of God.

CHILE AND PERU: FAMILY AND CELEBRATION

In Latin America we have made catechetical progress in the area of family and celebration (which are the two major thrusts of the realm of culture and efforts to inculturate). Let us look at two instances: a "family catechesis" that began in Chile and then spread through several areas of Latin America, and catechetical materials from the diocese of Cajamarca in Peru.[13]

Family catechesis is a predominantly urban evangelization. Adults, youths, and children have discussions intended to be used in setting up base communities, getting people involved in the parish, and giving Christian witness in society. It presents teaching in a salvation-history framework, and it is centered on Christ; it prepares adults and children for the sacraments, encourages family and social responsibility, and also includes intense moments of prayer and celebration.

I highlight three basic lines. One is healing in the family and building community. People evangelize themselves and inculturate the message in the midst of both conflict and harmony in the family. Another basic line is teaching and transforming life; it is not quick instruction in certain truths but a journey toward a Christocentric faith (in which a "passive and ritualistic religiosity" is sometimes challenged). The third line is celebrating faith. Over a two-year period of meetings with adults there are eleven celebrations and four get-togethers; each meeting of the children has moments for prayer, praise, joy, play, learning, and commitment.

Diocesan catechesis can be inculturated, as evidenced in Cajamarca in Peru. Materials have been prepared slowly and collaboratively, taking into account the living conditions and challenges of their context. People who are mainly peasants are taught the faith with images, prayers, and biblical readings. In the text for adults each chapter weaves together a case study, photo and drawing, discussion and questions, biblical material, singing and prayer, and invitation to action. The communal and family dimension are made more firm, and lay people are offered broad responsibilities (as was true of the previous case), particularly women. Salvation history is presented with a good pedagogy and doctrinal judgment.

These programs have excellent materials for aspects of worship and celebration: prayers and rosary, handbook of blessings, Marian novena, guide for rites of death, celebrations of Christian life. This directs inculturation along the path of sensitivity, spirituality, and commitment of the people. Symbols have a privileged place. It seems to me that more space could be given to the signs proper to each region, place, and human setting. It is with the eyes of the heart that one learns the message and sees the challenges of following Christ in today's world.

INCULTURATED CHALLENGES

The basic challenge is to be faithful to the command to evangelize (which includes doing catechesis) that Christ and his Spirit have imparted to the people of God, the church community. John Paul II has called us to a new evangelization, and in one of their decisions, the bishops agreed to do it in an inculturated manner. This concern is not limited to the present. An awareness of history shows us many excellent initiatives: faith shared in the family, currents of popular religiosity, official plans paying attention to the "signs of the times," inculturated specialized apostolic movements, base-communities, a range of movements of spirituality, contextualized and inculturated social action, programs to prepare for the sacraments, pastoral care at shrines, pastoral work in celebrations of the people. All this is encouraging and challenging, but much remains to be done. Each human sector has its needs and potentialities, where catechesis must continue to be done. I conclude by noting four challenges that in my view deserve greater attention.

The theological principles of inculturated catechesis. We have become accustomed to conceptualizing this work from the standpoint of Incarnation, but that is not enough. Catechesis is grounded on the entirety of revelation and the mystery of salvation. The church in Mexico and the CELAM agency have developed these foundations.[14] First there is the Trinity. Communication among the divine Persons is the source of our communication of faith among ourselves in love, and more specifically of a dialogical and community catechesis, with the mediation of Latin American values and cultural dynamics. The Christological foundation means that our sociocultural and personal processes are taken on and transformed by the Incarnation and Pasch of faith. The doctrine of Creation sheds light on all efforts at humanization; it also brings the ecological into catechesis. We know that pneumatology is the driving force of inculturation, from Pentecost until now. The mission of the church is carried out in all cultures and transcending them, with the methodology of interaction between the message and the real life of the people being catechized. The one driving this process is the Spirit who brings us to the truth. Furthermore, as M. Dhavamony has said,[15] the Christian message can be rethought in the categories of each culture. This entails transmitting the message in dialogue with each cultural process; inculturated theology is gradually taking shape in this journey.

Catechesis springs from the everyday and challenges it. Inculturation is not carried out with intellectual presentations on "the cultural." Through the principle of the interaction between faith and life developed in catechetics in Brazil and elsewhere in Latin America, all education of the faith is rooted in people's common concerns. That is, the message is relevant for our life, filled and overwhelmed as it is by conflicts, for every effort at humanization, for the advances and retreats in the everyday journey of the people. All human beings are called to conversion through their emotions, their struggle to live, their rituals and customs, the solidarity and hope around them. It is in relation to all of this that one is called to conversion and discipleship and to form part of the church community. There is no such thing as inculturated catechesis without this close systematic connection with the everyday. In its day-to-day life the community needs the fullness of the message, which is the gift of the Spirit.

The manifold unity of education in the faith. The church communicates and celebrates in the one God, the one who saves. All catechesis has this characteristic: engaging in dialogue about the mystery of salvation in history and hope in eternal life. This Christian salvation is what demands unity between Christians and members of other religions and nonbelievers. With regard to Catholic catechesis, we are called to unity in the church; its teaching has contents and methods that contribute to it. Yet there is a variety of forms of understanding and putting Christian faith in practice, inasmuch as we have a variety of symbolic universes and systems of knowledge. Historic and cultural situations make up part of the contents of catechesis; methodologies take age, region, sociocultural context, ecology, gender, and religious factors into account. Just as the Latin American population has many faces, so there are many modalities of inculturated catechesis, and they all flow together into the single route of salvation in Christ.

Teaching worked out in connection with the religion of humble people. This is a fourth great challenge. We receive and teach the faith on the basis of the rich experiences of God that abound in our continent, especially among the poor. The truth about Christ, the church, and the human being are also expressed in the language of the people's culture. The variety of rituals and feasts in every corner of Latin America hold sacramental treasures and a profound wisdom. This can be a part of catechesis. Grassroots religious organizations are spaces for catechesis with a great deal of lay responsibility and with inculturated ministries and charisms. The ethics of treating one's neighbor well, which is part of the religion of the poor, points toward the core of the Christian message. Yet the religiosity of ordinary people— like that of any group—has its ambiguities, its privatization, its sin; catechesis, therefore, evaluates and questions popular expressions.

A final word. The newness in this inculturated catechesis does not come from the thrust of modernity or from any pedagogical resources. What is new is the manifold work of the Spirit of Christ, received and taught in the Christian community. Also striking is the language of the poor, their faith and symbol system, their rationality and their hope, which become part of the teaching of the faith. The combination of the yearning for liberation with the enterprise of inculturation is another outstanding feature. As J. C. Scannone notes, "The evangelization of culture is not opposed to, but is intrinsically connected with, its option for the poor."[16] Making this a reality requires many joint efforts. One can see that a beginning has been made toward a fully inculturated catechesis in Latin America. That beginning may be hesitant but significant progress has been made and the route is laid out. With contributions from more communities and from those responsible for catechesis, and with greater creativity and less fear, further progress can be made.

4

Mission in the Life of the People

Over the course of five centuries of Christianity we have received waves of help from outside, and we have developed our own resources. Even though we are a colonized subcontinent, we are stirred by the irruption of the poor. Vatican II set forth new goals. Today, Latin America is sketching out its own vocation *ad gentes* inside the continent and elsewhere, one whose distinguishing feature is an "inculturated liberation."

What direction is mission taking today and tomorrow? The most obvious things is the journeying of communities: catechesis groups, bible circles, pastoral work of human rights, countless "popular Catholicism" associations, base Christian communities, and middle-class lay movements. All of them evangelize, build community, celebrate, pray, and heal; they all stand in solidarity with the cause of the poor, and they give and receive formation. There is a great deal of leadership by lay people, women, mestizo people, poor city dwellers, and youth. These situations call for a substantial rethinking of the contribution of men and women missionaries from other parts of the world to our "mission areas." Locally and regionally, opportunities are emerging for a new missionary phase in the characteristically Latin American "inculturated liberation" modality. It is about giving out of our poverty, evangelizing here and also in Asian and African environments.

The global and local context is very demanding. People in Latin America feel tugged in opposite directions by globalization and by their own energies. On a global scale, everything we do is dependent on the market, computerized information, consumer networks, standardized entertainment, science, and a utopia focused on individual advancement. And yet we are united by global links of another kind: celebration from within ourselves, a work ethic, ethnic reaffirmation, mixed economy, the pleasure of being with others, and emerging cultures.

What is happening to mission vis-à-vis these two overarching tendencies? Some approaches are personalistic: evangelize the human soul and

56

heart. They are being pursued internationally: evangelistic campaigns, the Catholic evangelization 2000 plan, the "electronic church" that is today the main means used by mission. These are First World and (supposedly) apolitical directions that seek to redeem modernity. On the other hand we have a many-sided creative mission carried out by Christian communities teeming with signs of life and a genuine humanization. It is here that the church of the poor (and of all) is taking hold. Mission generally fluctuates between these two poles: one of them neocolonial and leveling, and the other driven by the "least ones" with their catholic and inculturating qualities.

Even though diplomatic language may be used (missionary activity, witnessing the faith), actually representatives of Christian denominations compete aggressively. We believers who invoke the same God of Jesus Christ are continually acting in a proselytizing way and with a missiology that denies the "other." We cultivate the sin of exclusion and a doctrinaire spirit. Within the Catholic church in Latin America, moreover, we sometimes tend to work against one another, grassroots initiatives are mistrusted, and predictions that by the year 2000 half the people will be Protestant are causing panic. Ugly battles take place on the terrain of religion. Nevertheless, I think that the greatest devastation is wrought by our sacralized world. Indeed, the "good news" of progress has its "mission" of granting happiness and success. Although most of the people receive only crumbs, they are seduced by modernity. Secular "success" both arouses enthusiasm and causes frustration, and makes millions of people live in illusions. Its offer of a transcendental happiness seems to be the main opponent with whom the Christian message has to contend. Mission therefore unfolds in the midst of highly conflictive and complicated contexts.

In these post-council years many efforts have been made to reformulate mission—with realism and freedom of spirit.[1] The reformulation is being proposed on the basis of the gospel tradition, and it is nourished by spirituality. Ultimately, mission is fruit of the movement of the Spirit given to the people of God. This movement is quite different from plans of a church turned in on itself. Our accent is placed on the work of the Spirit, who renews the evangelizing service toward humankind that hungers for God.

TRENDS AND PROSPECTS

Evangelizing activity is carried out and understood in many ways. My first experience was as a layman in a peasant settlement in Talca, Chile; I sought to teach those who were "ignorant." Later on, as a religious in urban settings, I took on the standpoint of evangelizing through consciousness-raising and the observe-judge-act method. Today, with indigenous, farmers, and small merchants (in Chucuito, Peru) I understand mission as accompaniment and celebration. Over the years (which help us to mature our approaches and to adjust methods) many of us have tried various approaches to evangelization.

In overall terms, what is happening in our continent?

CHURCH IN MOVEMENT

Mission is generally understood in a restricted sense as a specialized work in geographical places and in human areas where there is no ecclesiastical presence. It is a work carried out by the "more educated" coming from Latin American cities and from overseas who bring with them an economic dependency that is constraining. (Hence, there would seem to be no place for mission in a community that had self-generated personnel and material means.)

A broader and more traditional understanding is that of a movement, as is indicated by the term in Latin: *missio*. It is the action of sending, and the unfolding of a task; it is going as one sent and performing activities. In other words, mission is a process that is part of all evangelization carried out by the church at the service of the salvation of humankind.[2] One of its modalities is that of a plan and special mission period in the diocese and parish, carried out primarily by lay leaders.

Mission has various levels of meaning. It has a theological content because God and God's church are in movement and at the service of the whole human being and of the regeneration of the cosmos. It also has an organizational meaning: missionary programs carried out by dioceses, religious orders and congregations, lay movements, base communities, and agencies of "popular Catholicism." It also has family, economic, political, and ideological components, which are inseparable from the foregoing. Hence, it would be shortsighted to focus only on what has to do with matters inside the church; for example, the action of foreign missionaries and spiritual benefits acquired by those to whom the mission is addressed.

Mission forms part of the church's entire endeavor and identity; its doctrinal solidity must be accompanied by competent performance in terms of organization, communications, economics, and training. It is a mission movement; it is a movement of inculturating liberation. This perspective is rooted in Vatican II. It has to do with the entire activity of the church (AG 5) and not simply with converting pagans and expanding church boundaries. It has stages of "planting," "young church," and "local church" (AG 6). At a deeper level, it is about "sacramental mission" (LG 1-3).

In our situations of impoverishment and violence, where people are also taking initiatives and affirming their culture, what form does mission take with its problems and opportunities? Let us review some basic issues.

Latin Americans are subjected to contradictory Christian messages. Indeed, many people are targeted for mission conquest. Methods abound for setting up opposition based on fear ("us" and "them," salvation or eternal condemnation, prepare for the end of the world) by conservative sects and churches. Sectarian and unecumenical attitudes and authoritarian models are often presented as features of the gospel, when they are actually devices for social, cultural, and spiritual control.

Voices of alarm are being raised in institutions: the number of people who are insufficiently evangelized and unbelieving is rising; and the number of missionaries, both foreign and domestic, is declining. Nevertheless, what seems much more problematic to me is the lack of communication between Christian bodies, their competitiveness, and the lack of attention to the syncretistic experiences of the mestizo, indigenous, and Afro-America majorities. Another great issue is that mission goes hand in hand with "Christian civilization." In this regard J. Daniélou used to say that only the Catholic religion was instituted by God. Other religions are produced by human beings. He also said that Christianity unifies Western civilization.[3] A mission crusade toward Latin America has been carried out from the United States.[4] It is plain to see that missionary behavior is infected by imperial-cultural activity.

Taking such issues into account, what are missionary opportunities today? I think that the primary opportunity is the spread of Latin American styles and objectives: inculturated liberation. Who is putting it into practice? Primarily the laity, poor Christian communities, religious men and women living among the people, and vicariates and dioceses with missionary plans. It is also in our hands to build a real ecumenism, not only between Christian groups and expressions, but with the religions of the people (which until now have been classified as superstitions and as incomplete forms of Christianity).

In theological expression there are certain either/ors that are disturbing to people. Pitting efforts to convert non-Catholics and refraining from mission because salvation is universal is a false split. God unquestionably offers salvation to all, and yet the church calls each human being to become part of the people of God. These things are not contradictory. Nor is it necessary to chose between the particular notion of a missionary in areas scarcely reached by the church and the notion that the entire church engages in mission. Both are necessary and mutually complementary.

MISSION MODELS

We know that Catholic individuals and groups cover a wide range. They can be summed up in the following models:

- mission imparts true knowledge; this objective is generally pursued ethnocentrically, because evangelizers coming from "developed" cultures go out to change marginal cultures;
- mission encourages reception of sacraments and popular devotions, thereby often leading to sectarian behavior; those who respond to these mission offers are regarded as "faithful" and others have to be incorporated into "our" mission;

- mission confronts secularism and injects transcendence; this is the mission objective in neo-Christendom circles, in their pursuit of a new civilization of love, which sometimes comes down to forging a Christian-modern-mestizo culture;
- mission carried out by ecclesial communities, convoked and sent by the Holy Spirit; their option for the poor may be carried out in an inculturating and liberating manner (although sometimes it is posed unilaterally and does not encompass the evangelization of the entire person and of the full unfolding of the human). Catholicity requires giving testimony to the salvation of persons in all cultures, which entails an eschatological critique of each of them.

These models may be summarized as:

Mission goal	Human action
1. rational teaching	neo-colonization
2. strengthening pastoral activity	sectarian groups
3. faith in the context of modernity	creating Christian culture
4. community according to the Spirit	inculturated liberation

The first three enjoy a great deal of institutional backing. Models 2 and 4 are more in agreement with the Christian experiences of the bulk of the people. The last one seems to be most in tune with Latin American tradition and its reading of the gospel; this community-oriented model moreover includes the other concerns: teaching, cultivating the faith and praying, and offering modernity a message.

These models of mission have their historic trajectories; these paths have been followed over many generations and they represent the sacrificial endeavors of countless people. A missiological reflection entails evaluating Latin American legacies from the past.[5]

The repercussions of the complex colonial legacy, which developed from the sixteenth century to the nineteenth, continue up to the present. Neo-colonial versions connect mission with those who wield power in modernity. For example, much mission planning stresses training a few elites so that they can lead the rest of the population.

Starting in the nineteenth century, mission tended to be dissociated from such powers and to concentrate on the church structure. Protestantism entered Latin America, initially spreading slowly and in a limited way. Catholic work was carried out primarily by religious orders and congregations with help from Europe. Then, during the twentieth century, evangelical and pentecostal denominations (which in a few decades became the majority expression of Protestantism, partly because of an intense inculturation) took hold and spread in popular sectors. Their vitality competed with Catholic evangelization. Both are focused on worship: the praying evangelical community or Mass attendance, sacraments, and devotional events. In the mid-twentieth century energetic contingents of men and women missionaries from North America and Europe arrived and helped modernize Catholic mission.

In general, these legacies coexist alongside one another, even though they are quite distinct. We need only compare our situation with the rapid decolonization of Africa and Asia from the 1940s to the 1960s, a process that meant that Christian mission, which had been sustained from Europe, had to be completely rethought. It is noteworthy that in the past few decades trends toward neocolonization have worsened in Latin America, thereby making it even more difficult for our own homegrown mission and communion in shared responsibility with other churches.

Another important legacy is that of believing communities and of men and women missionaries who are fully committed to the cause of the continent's poor. Here liberation theology has borne fruit. In this connection it is well to be reminded that from the outset bringing people to the faith has included inculturated forms in solidarity. That is how mission has been carried out for five centuries by Christian families, by popular devotions, by organizers of religious celebrations, by all kinds of Catholic groups. In short, persons and communities, laity and hierarchy, have been witnesses and communicators of the gift of salvation with some degree of inculturation.

Taken altogether, these legacies are now facing the challenge of delineating mission at the service of poor and deeply believing peoples. Vatican Council II has defined the content of this renewal: to be church-sacrament of universal salvation. Hence, mission entails full liberation. It is not mission-for-self or to coerce nonbelievers, or simply to expand church power. One asks: How are we to be signs of the salvation of humankind in Latin America? The best response is given by poor communities; they are the midwives of the mission that liberates on the basis of each people's project of life (of culture). Communities do this insofar as they are faithful to the gospel tradition and to the extent that their ecclesial identity is truly one of service.

TRADITIONAL INNOVATION

Opportunities for renewing mission are emerging and expanding on all sides. It is sad to see that they do not come out of missiological reflection, because it remains limited to pastoral agents in designated "mission" zones. Likewise, there is little innovation by the so-called mission works in each local church. I see greater creativity in everyday evangelization through certain specific priorities.

LATIN AMERICAN PRIORITIES

How is the post-Easter commission—"Go and make disciples of all people" (Mt 28:19), "Go through the world and announce the good news"

(Mk 16:15)—put into practice in Latin America today? It seems to me that we put it in practice along two main lines.

One great pastoral priority is service to poor, marginalized people in the city, especially work with youth, women, education, and popular organizing. Because of the vast migration taking place since the mid-twentieth century, missionary resources have turned toward the marginalized urban population. A second primary line of work is the range of priorities in Amazon, indigenous, peasant, mestizo, and Afro-American settings. In mission terms, they are all manifestations of the option for the poor.

Recently, other lines of work are being added. Lively lay movements are engaging in mission, primarily in middle- and upper-class milieux. Also taking root is a proposal to work together with other poor peoples of the world where Christianity is in a minority (Asia) or where it is expanding (Africa); these proposals are being driven by missionary congresses (COMLAs) in Latin America.

Alongside these four positive thrusts are huge gaps. Neither the valiant option from among the poor nor the manifold task of inculturation has taken hold in the everyday movement of the church and its structures. There is very little missionary presence in the mass media (where the prevailing tendency is the "good news" of materialistic progress and a fundamentalist "electronic church"). Likewise obvious are failures in the education system (which is discriminatory and denies cultural particularities within each national state). In short, we have become accustomed to a state of confusion. On the one hand, we have outstanding examples of gospel motivations and generous efforts by many missionary staff members. On the other hand, there are negative plans: a neo-Christendom framework, acceptance of the demands of democratic capitalism, and the project of integrating (rather than transforming) Latin America. There is a great need to shed light on the social and political conditions of missionary endeavor, as well as to review the priorities listed above. On the basis of what criteria? With those of Christian tradition. "Going out to the entire world" is not enough; in doing so we must be guided by the Spirit and be disciples of the missionary Jesus with, and out of, the poor.

All over the continent those who are most intensively carrying out Christ's mission are weak and insignificant people. They do so with vigor and with a marvelous spirituality. Our eyes are thereby opened to the tradition.

The New Testament narratives portray marginal people as bearers of the mission, and the Spirit of the Risen One as the one leading evangelization. Specifically, we find Jesus—educated in the home of a carpenter—and fisherfolk by a lake, women faithful to the master, many sick people, and converted sinners. We are also struck by how Jesus rejects the devil's temptations to act with extraordinary powers. The first communities are made up of male and female disciples, who have no claims to being wise, who have no material or political privileges.

This way of working is summed up by St. Paul with paradoxical words: doing mission comes out of weakness. That is, one who is insignificant and weak is truly able to carry out mission. Paul even attributes weakness to God; such weakness is stronger than human self-aggrandizement. Believers are likewise weak, but that is the condition in which God has chosen them, and so God confounds the strong (see 1 Cor 1:25-27). This is also a feature of the missionary: "we are weak, you are strong"; "To the weak I became weak to win over the weak" (1 Cor 4:10, 9:22, 2 Cor 11:30). It is just such weak persons (from despised cultures) that the Spirit strengthens and sends out.

It is unquestionably God who directs the work. The Spirit of the Risen One stirs up witness "to the ends of the earth" (Acts 1:8). In this regard it is striking that witness was done by believers from Jewish and pagan cultures. Acts offers us two scenes of Pentecost. In one the Jews accept the Spirit and launch the mission to all cultures ("other languages" [Acts 2:1-24]). In the other Pentecost, the gift of the Spirit is received by Gentiles, who also speak in tongues and glorify God (see Acts 10:44-47, 11:15, 15:8-9). In the Gentile and lay community in Antioch the community imposes hands on two who are chosen by the Spirit and sends them out to engage in mission (Acts 13:1-4).

Thus, people who are insignificant, weak, poor, and despised are those whom the Spirit chooses and commissions for the work of God on this earth. It is that very tradition that comes alive in local churches in Latin America, where "little ones" and the outcast, women, young people, blacks, indigenous, mestizos, the ill (and their cultural environments) are weak— yet competent in the mission of the Lord. If that is so, why is mission often headed by the "educated" from the upper-middle and upper classes? We are inconsistent.

MISSION FOR THE REIGN

What is mission for? Not for being honored within it or outside it. It is a service to the reign, in order to be faithful to the Spirit of God. This is the meaning of discipleship, the very raison d'etre of the church, which is the sacrament of God's saving love.

It is no exaggeration to say that such practices, inspired by the Spirit and at the service of the reign, abound in Latin American churches. However, there are also other currents that characteristically continue as a church connected to power; in the area of content, they seek to make Christ known. The problem is that this message, which is good in itself, is disfigured and trapped by the powers and the logic of this world; it is also problematic to say that those who know certain things are evangelized.

Let us relocate ourselves in the founding mission. Jesus and his Spirit establish mission for the sake of conversion from sin, observance of love, sacramental community, witness to the Pasch of Christ. All of this has a basic orientation: movement in terms of the reign. Doing mission thus means placing oneself in this movement.

This process is initiated and sustained by God, a process in which the persons sent and those who help in mission are transformed and also set in motion. Jesus, a wanderer, claims that the reign is near at hand and hence substantial changes are also near (see Mk 1:14-15, Lk 4:16-22, Mt 45:22-25). He announces the reign and heals sicknesses; the reign demands belief and a change in one's life direction. It is accepted by those made sorrowful and trampled upon; to them it provides joy and freedom. Into these dynamics enter the Twelve and persons who are disciples. The apostolic group, having neither gold nor silver, is sent out to announce the reign, perform healing, expel demons, and grant peace, but they suffer assaults (Mt 10:1-33). Jesus also charges the seventy-two disciples to go humbly, proclaiming that the reign is near, to heal the sick and share peace (Lk 10:1-12). That is the direction their work takes after Pentecost; so say the apostles in their proclamation (Acts 1:3, 14:22, 19:8, 28:23) and when they use images of entering the reign. People are set in motion, fired up by the presence of God in the midst of his people, and that entails a most intense service to the needy and to each believer. This is not a blandly bureaucratic endeavor. Quite the contrary, it is a decisive, charismatic movement, obedient to the Spirit, defined by the proximity and impact of the reign. Mission may be described as "passionate" for God's reign.

When one examines the generous evangelization carried out in Latin America, what stands out are signs of warm fidelity to the reign promised to the impoverished. This is a most important topic in the teaching of the faith. It also characterizes social action and solidarity in the cause of the poor. It is evident as ministry and charism around illness and healing, around violence and their "evil spirits." But not all is well. There is also a tendency to associate some human achievements with what is assumed to be God's providence; for example, projects of modern neo-Christendom (such as creating a Christian culture), or tying ecclesial mission to a "Latin American integration" whose spokespersons come from the elite. These tendencies come not from the weak in the strength of the Spirit but from ambiguous social and religious powers.

ECCLESIAL INNOVATION

The guidelines of mission changed over the twentieth century. I am going to recall some of those guidelines. In 1919 Benedict XV expressed the classic concern for "souls." In his 1951 and 1957 encyclicals Pius XII called for the expansion of a neo-Christendom church that entailed a Christian social order.[6] Vatican Council II is now our major guideline. It presented the entire church within human history as missionary. This position stands in contrast to what had preceded: Christian areas used to send missionaries to "save souls" in pagan regions. Today the church, "in solidarity with humankind and its history" (GS 1 and 11), engages in mission in accordance with the "design of God and its fulfillment in the world and in world history" (AG 9). All believers, dioceses, and ministries are regarded as missionary (AG 35-41); it is a universal endeavor "to all human beings and peoples to lead them to faith, freedom, and peace in Christ" (AG 5; LG 16-17). There are also "missions" in the special sense: "Preaching the gospel and setting up the church among peoples or groups who do not yet believe in Christ" (AG 6, 7, 10, 19, 23-24). Everything is based on the Trinitarian mission, the mission of Christ by the Holy Spirit (AG 2-4).

Another guideline is the renewed papal teaching on evangelization and mission *ad gentes*. In *Evangelii Nuntiandi* Paul VI reiterated that the entire church is missionary (59-61) in every setting and people (18, 49-58). Mission entails cultural aspects (20-23) and especially liberating aspects (30-39); this latter is at the heart of the church, and the former is necessary (that is why I use the phrase *inculturated liberation*). The action of the Holy Spirit is also noteworthy: "[the] principal agent of evangelization . . . who stirs up the new . . . humanity of which evangelization is to be the result" (75). The prophetic *Redemptoris Missio* (1990) of John Paul II contains the great themes of mission, and they are grounded in a novel way in the perspective of the reign (chap. 2) and of the Spirit (chap. 3). The church is "dynamic power in the journey of humankind toward the Reign" (20); the Spirit of God is "active protagonist of the entire ecclesial mission" and at work in every time and place (21, 28). Our shepherd also insists on the permanent validity of *ad gentes* (1-3, 31-34), and includes new social and cultural realities, youth, mass media, and especially the needs of the South and the East in today's world. This renewed vision has been maturing in many places, as evidenced by the international SEDOS conference (Rome, 1981), at which an agenda for the future of mission was laid out: proclamation, dialogue, interculturation, liberation.[7]

In Latin American terms the guideposts of Medellín, Puebla, and Santo Domingo press forward specific commitments and bold proposals. In going over the texts one finds key facets. A renewing vision is raised by the bishops gathered in Medellín, Puebla, and Santo Domingo (hereafter M, P, and SD), and by the prophetic events organized by the CELAM Department of Missions: Melgar (1968) and Manaus (1977).[8] In continuity with the council, mission is understood as the endeavor of all: laity (M-liturgy 3 and 6, P 9, 363, 655, 712, 806); the parish (SD 58); priests and bishops (M-priests 17, P 686, 712); men and women religious (M-rel. 4 and 13, P 755, 773); women (SD 90); youth (SD 111); and as specific work (M-popular pastoral work 15; P 363, 368, 1010). It is also described in terms of liberation (P 368, 1304). We thus have an accent on ecclesial collaboration, carried out in service to the call to universal salvation, of which the church is sacrament.

A further aspect of mission is its community nature, whether in the powerful expressions of popular Catholicism, which spread the faith among countless groups of people, or in specialized expressions (lay movements, bible circles, base Christian communities) that nourish a deepening of the message and of the mission endeavor. In this regard remarkable work is done by "small communities [which] live the faith in close community of life and with a missionary projection" (SD 48). Likewise outstanding is the work of religious congregations in Latin America; as community they evangelize in the fields of education, health, parish, and in the various worlds of the poor.

A third facet is the stance of dialogue with other cultures and religions. We no longer go out to rescue "souls" from paganism; rather, our effort is to enter into communion with every human being and, as Puebla put it, to "give from our own poverty" (368), and, as was agreed upon at COMLA-4, to give priority to the encouragement, training, and missionary organization of the entire people of God with something quite new, namely, entering into dialogue with other peoples and cultures.[9] This point is extremely important.

Specifically missiological teaching and thinking are still incipient in Latin America,[10] but great progress has been made in the ecclesiology of opting for the poor and their cultures, and out of those cultures, accepting the Word and living the paschal mystery. This perspective has Trinitarian, sacramental, and pneumatological accents.

God, community, and communication of persons and of the missions of the Son and the Spirit are conceived in terms of mission. As L. Boff explains, the Trinitarian reality is not centered on self, inasmuch as the Father sends the Son to "make all human beings sons and daughters" and the Spirit to "enspirit humankind."[11] The idea of *missio Dei* has to do with the divinity and its relationship with evangelizing action, because the Trinity is present in each concrete mission that we carry out. Moreover, as Gustavo Gutiérrez points out, mission in Latin America is characterized by the option for the poor, for martyrdom, and for being subjects "with much to contribute" by way of our own experiences and thinking.[12] Speaking generally, mission comes from God and is placed at the service of salvation from sin and of the experience of love, with all its implications in our situation.

The sacramental accent has to do with the heart of ecclesial mission: being a sign of integral liberation and of salvation from sin. It is the experience of the believing community. When we receive the sacraments (baptism, confirmation, anointing of the sick, reconciliation, eucharist, matrimony, and orders), we are sent forth to give witness and to share saving grace with our neighbors. In addition, there exists a many-sided popular Catholicism with countless ministries and sacramentals that point to God's work at every moment and every place in our lives. Besides that, there are syncretisms with Christian ingredients and elements from other symbolic worlds, where many people find signs of God's love. In short, missiology is alert to the everyday symbols of salvation that people find within our church circles and beyond them. These symbols are nourished by every culture.

We are well aware that all of mission is defined by the charismatic (even though that notion is misused by some evangelical and Catholic circles). Pneumatology has marvelous implications in our situations of cultural and religious pluralism. Vatican II proposed not simply "adaptation" but an "exchange between gospel and cultures" (GS 44; AG 22), with which there can be "diversity in unity" (AG 22). There is more, however. Non-Christian environments are not devoid of the Spirit. "The presence and activity of the Spirit . . . affects societies, history, peoples, cultures, and religions" (*Redemptoris Missio* 28). Out of Latin America we call for an "encounter in dialogue with the other religions and cultures of the world—where the Spirit is at work—in order to bring them into the fullness of the gospel" (COMLA-4). If this teaching is put into effect, mission methodology will be utterly different from what prevailed in the past. The point now is not to replace religions (colonial method) or to tolerate other religions and adapt the message to each culture (method during modernity). It is now possible to evangelize in consonance with the signs of the Spirit in each human process. This is unquestionably a qualitative advance.

INCULTURATED LIBERATION

In Latin America with its many facets we have a broad goal that can be described as *inculturated liberation*. Reassuming the positive traditions of the continent, it energizes each area of mission: proclamation, liturgy, teaching, church administration, social action, and spiritual witness. But this goal is sometimes manipulated like a banner or is limited to talk rather than being patiently put into practice. How are we to assure that it functions as a goal? We can plainly see that this happens insofar as it is put into practice by communities that are poor and missionary.

This proposal was conceived some twenty years ago and was soon baptized at the Puebla conference in 1979. Our mission *ad gentes* is to give something original out of our poverty: a sense of liberation-salvation, popular religiosity, base Christian community, ministries, hope and joy (368). We may also specify its human agents: Christian communities, generally poor, are those who engage in mission here and elsewhere in the world.

We are not beginning from scratch. For five hundred years Christian families and communities have engaged in mission. Can they now do so with greater intensity and universality? For centuries they have contributed with their community mode of life, healing (in all senses) sick people, shared celebration, grassroots leaders, and the morality of welfare for all. These missionary capabilities and gifts have been exercised by people who are weak—as were Jesus, his apostles, Mary, the disciples, and Paul. Those who are socially and religiously outcast have been the driving force of mission.

Again, I insist that this has been happening for centuries. It did not begin twenty years ago when pastoral specialists proposed mission *ad extra* from

Latin America. But it can be reformulated, thanks to the self-esteem of the poor and an agenda of inculturation. This must take place within our continent, which hungers for evangelization, and also elsewhere on the globe. The underlying issues are paradoxical. Those who give most and in the best spirit are those in need. As R. Aubry states, "We have gotten used to thinking that the rich give and the poor receive. But it is the poor who give."[13] And it is those who are so often classified as insufficiently civilized who contribute most to inculturating the gospel.

This is not only phenomenologically evident but is a theological fact. Thank God, the church of the poor is exceedingly generous and manifests various degrees of inculturation. It transmits the faith from generation to generation, in far-off places and in our huge cities. It provides consolation; it communicates its popular grasp of the Word and its veneration of icons; it organizes the church from the grassroots; it develops countless forms of ministry; it has an ethic of solidarity; and much more happens in every hamlet in our continent. This church of the poor is also beginning to send religious, laity, and priests to other countries. (At the same time, well-financed groups with many people are now reestablishing a neocolonial type of mission.)

Mission within and out of poor communities takes into account the "signs of the times." In East Asia it is primarily pentecostal denominations that are bringing about the main torrent of conversion and life in community. In Africa, many new, so-called independent churches (out of colonialism) that have selected Christian traditions relevant to their own cultures are multiplying. Millions of Catholics in Latin America are entering Christian denominations and sects that offer them better sociocultural and spiritual service.[14] These phenomena have many variables and may be interpreted in a number of ways, but each of them exhibits effective ways of inculturation. We find effective social and cultural expressions of communication with God, community, healing, experience of the Spirit. These "signs of the times" are an invitation to us to rethink and revise our Catholic mission.

Let us return to the heart of the Latin American proposal, which connects two dimensions: liberation and inculturation. Liberation is a living experience that is both comprehensive and concrete. It has to do with the small and large achievements of communities becoming more human (in soteriological terms, persons and communities finding salvation from evil and sin). The second dimension is that each community and people, with its cultural paths, internalizes the message and puts it into practice. This inculturation also confronts local customs that cause our self-destruction and the almost omnipotent overarching culture of the market and the individual. This linkage reflects the sense of the believing community and was spelled out in the early 1980s by Paulo Suess: a "theological vision combining inculturation and liberation."[15]

The basis for this linkage is faith in God who loves humankind and liberates it; this takes place within each person and culture. Unfortunately, the idea of liberation has been disfigured as something that is partial (social structures, psychological structures, personal sin) and characteristic of progressive elites (those who have clear ideas, or greater spirituality, or who are more organized). That is not what it is about. Liberating mission is holistic; it is neither determinism nor fantasy. Nor is the notion of inculturation restricted to what is usually called cultural; it embraces all human reality and its surroundings, and it responds to the work of the Spirit of Christ, who inspires every person and every people, on the basis of their own symbolic universe, to become responsible for the gospel. Hence, this is not a pastoral tactic of becoming incarnate to utilize and retrieve some items of culture. Nor is it a kind of cultural totalitarianism, in which everything is seen as cultural, and that would be the deepest level of reality. In short, inculturation is a process carried out by each ecclesial community that accepts the Spirit, who challenges its cultural processes.

Who, today and tomorrow in our continent, is driving liberating and inculturated mission? It is the members of the church present in the midst of different human realms, and especially present in urban poor sectors with their emerging cultures, and in mestizo, indigenous, and black settings. At the Santo Domingo Conference, emphasis was placed on inculturation in (and implicitly inculturating mission carried out by) indigenous, mestizo, and Afro-American groups and those that are part of modernity (see SD 252-262, 243-251). The potential of these human sectors is great. I am thinking particularly of marginal young people (almost half the population of Latin America and the Caribbean); in the midst of their ambivalences, advances and retreats, authenticity and mimicry, they can give a new direction to church mission. Likewise, the gender perspective as elaborated by women and more recently by men, enabling mission to be healthily relational and not excluding, is ever more significant. It is foreseeable that the next missionary stage in Latin America will be enriched by the energies of young people and by different contributions by men and women in shared mission. In terms of participation by the people of God, those who can best drive mission forward are those who have an ecumenical spirituality and practice; in each church the lay community united to the hierarchical authority that serves communion is missionary.

In emphasizing the mission of the entirety of the people of God, the obvious limitations in all its members must not be ignored. Neither the people nor the poor, neither those responsible for the church nor the base community, should be absolutized. No one is author of all truth and good. Nor may talents and intellectual gifts of missionary individuals and the episcopate be made sacrosanct. Each and every one of us needs salvation, and by faith and love we receive it. It is not a human work; missionary vocation and perseverance is a gift. In these pages the active role of poor communities has been emphasized. They are—like everyone else—fallible and sinful, and they engage in mission only insofar as they are disciples of the Lord and faithful to his Spirit. Otherwise, one would be uncritically supporting every belief and action of the Christian people. Indeed inculturation is not an objective and static thing but a process. As David Bosch notes, "one may never use the term 'inculturated,'" because what we have is a cultural process and because the church can be led to new dimensions of the faith.[16] One is thus always on the way to inculturation and never finishes this endeavor; inculturated mission is always open to discovering new facets of the Mystery.

This experience is basically about the *missio Dei*. The Trinity as community of Persons redeeming humankind is missionary (as Clodomiro Siller notes in Mexico). Jesus and his disciples announced the reign and were led by the Spirit, so mission today and tomorrow in Latin America is in keeping with the presence of the reign and the impulse of the Spirit (as stressed in the missiology of J. Comblin, L. A. Castro, M. Pozo, R. Aubry, and others). Likewise, many are suggesting that we are beginning to accept the grace of the missionary *kairos*. This moment of grace is not so that we may be puffed up, but rather its meaning is that of service: "If the church in Latin America goes beyond its borders, it is to be the church of the Risen Lord who wishes to form his body with all the peoples of the earth."[17] As I have explained in the course of these pages, it is a mission in the Spirit carried out by communities of faith, primarily the poor and those enriched by their popular Christianity.

These theological guidelines entail methodologies created within each people by the local church. For example, a good Christological pedagogy does not exclude or push aside the religion of the people. Biblical catechesis draws nourishment from Latin American beliefs linked to images of Christ and Mary. Inculturated missionary activity is also in dialogue with syncretistic symbol systems.[18] A crucial point is not to reject but rather to draw on and make known syncretistic forms as the poor majority handles illnesses and obtains health. These practices are correlated with the message of salvation.

Another very demanding matter is that of shaping a life-project, that is, the relationship between Christian mission and bringing about a positive world based on today's potentialities. In past decades attempts were made at a model of Christian presence and mission in the midst of organizations and large-scale social change. Today other models are being attempted: small everyday contributions to the globalization of hope, connection between praxis and celebration, strengthening the family and local groups, a kind of production and consumption that is an alternative to a totalitarian market, art and ecology, responsibility of people's organizations to resolve matters of the common good. These may be regarded as seeds of a life-project in human history, evoked by the promises of the reign. We are already living it, and yet we are not!

In conclusion, our missionary *kairos* in Latin America bears the stamp of inculturated liberation both inside our continent and outside it. Its theological supports are the reign and the work of the Spirit. This drive is led by the church of the poor, which is the teacher of inculturation. It is a global movement aimed at a freedom that is anticipated and celebrated at each moment and every place in the human pilgrimage. There is no such thing as what is properly missionary (for example, sacraments and catechesis) and what is secondary and preparatory for mission (for example, social action, education). Everything forms part of the movement of mission, and the whole of mission offers concrete signs of liberation. These signs are present in kerygmatic proclamation, in the development of the inculturated church, in healing and celebration, in solidarity ethics, and in teaching the truth, in everyday organization and in spirituality. Thus unfolds the mission that we share with the Spirit of God.

5

Religion of the Poor

Christian communities are bearers and teachers of a faith inculturated in a variety of ways. Yet they also produce dehumanizing religious forms (which are commonly called Christian). In other words, there are contradictions within the religions of a people carrying out inculturation. There are also controversies, because there are various types of inculturated faith; for example, the clash between those who cultivate devotions and those who are in official leadership positions and base communities, between members of Christian denominations whose social and cultural ways of expressing their faith are different, between those who defend ancestral customs and young people with their religiosity of progress. Hence, multifaceted and complex "popular religion" gives rise to many kinds of inculturation and controversies over them. These tensions do not simply arise over specific areas of belief and doctrine but also tensions over different ways of living the faith due to different emotional, economic, political, and cultural backgrounds. Church bodies, on the other hand, tend to dismiss the Christianities of the common people, calling them mere religiosity (which needs to be evangelized) or mere cultural expression. When such bodies speak of inculturated pastoral activity they disregard the wise inculturations already performed by the people.

Hence, I begin this chapter by emphasizing disputes and contending positions, so we will not enter the topic of inculturated Latin American Christianities ingenuously. I also take note of the relevance of the topic for our present age of social and political skepticism, and intellectual uncertainty over the possibility of building something new. In these difficult settings the inculturated Christian community can teach us about quality of human life and specific alternatives.

CLARIFICATIONS

An issue as broad and difficult as this needs some initial clarifications in both theory and practice. At the outset I emphasize that the inculturation of

Christianity takes place in all dimensions of life; it is not circumscribed to what is intrinsically religious. Unfortunately many reduce it to ritual, artistic, or conceptual matters. I am going to consider one aspect of historic development in our continent: the inculturated Christianities that have been elaborated among poor populations. This has to do with seeing reality from and out of "those at the bottom," and doing so with the striving for liberation that is part of the gospel given to those who are "least" on the earth. To consider here all the religious systems existing in Latin America (which displays a mosaic of inculturations) would be impossible. I limit myself to the terrain of Catholicisms lived by the people.

THEORETICAL QUESTIONS

Briefly, I take up three fundamental questions: human ambivalence, the vision of history, and today's cultures.

Human processes are polyvalent and ambivalent. I am not going to assume unreal dualisms where one factor excludes the other. For example, it is not realistic to imagine one inculturation carried out by hegemonic sectors and another carried out by the oppressed, just as it is not realistic to propose that there is an official religion over against a popular religion. Such dualisms and others like them do not capture the interaction between nuanced and complex realities, among social groups, among cultural universes. Obviously, in the entire human condition—and in the area of inculturation as well—there is a great deal of ambivalence. It is thus worthwhile critically to examine these human processes, without assuming that some are correct and positive or that others are incorrect and negative.

Another clarification has to do with what is historical. What vision of history best enables us to understand the inculturation carried out by ordinary people? If we classify periods into ancient (premodern), medieval (which for us has meant colonialism), and modern, the criteria of the latter tend to be privileged. This evolutionary classification is unable to explain particular histories in our continent. Nor does it value the experiences of faith—and inculturation—before the arrival of Christianity. Another problematic issue is isolating scholarly history, which would establish and interpret the factual, from a faith perspective, which sees salvation history; in doing so, the religious dimension is separated from human process, and not all levels of an inculturated phenomenon are grasped. To me, it seems preferable to examine what happens in the everyday life of the believing population, taking into account human processes and the popular experience of faith that touch all aspects of reality. The unfolding of events can be read in a critical and humanistic way (in keeping with scholarly standards) and in a believing and theological way (from within the experience of the people of God and with theological criteria).

Yet another issue is what is happening on the contemporary cultural scene. Many analysts emphasize planetary globalization, which calls into question small local and regional cultures. We are unquestionably in the midst of a cultural and ethical revolution that is worldwide in scope; the global and the local are interconnected. Latin American peoples are both claiming their own features and assuring that they participate in the universal. There are contacts, conflicts, and connections among life systems. We have various ways of being inserted into global dynamics and degrees of relative autonomy vis-à-vis modern civilization. Moreover, our continent has a range of identities: several kinds of mestizajes, Afro-American, Amerindian, Asian American populations, middle classes, and pro–first-world elites. These identities are very much marked by the context of progress and by science and technology, by frustrated illusions, by the emergence of masses of young people, and by exclusion from many of the goods and services of the contemporary world. The scene is full of contradictions and overflowing with anguish. Xavier Gorostiaga notes that the market "offers a future full of promises but with no project and no hope."[1] Within this scene we often observe psychosocial evasion, fundamentalisms that offer security, and symptomatic identification with successful personalities. Thus there are many mechanisms of illusory happiness seeking to overcome widespread frustration. This is the cultural stage on which inculturation unfolds.

PRACTICAL MATTERS

Along with contexts and process, let us briefly look at some practical matters: the impact of youth on inculturation, religious modernization, syncretism, interreligious matters, religious legitimation of power—and finally, the ecclesial aspect.

In our continent young people are the main bearers of and challenge to inculturated religious experiences. This is the case even though many young people are indifferent, and even irreverent, toward church matters. I am not setting the world of the young apart from that of adults. But I do want to insist that religious changes are in the hands of poor and believing youth; it is they who lay out the direction toward inculturation. Popular religion is often considered something proper to adults and static social sectors, but in our countries what stands out is the initiative of emerging groups, such as young people. For example, they go to many shrines, and they wear various amulets. The impact of youth on the mosaic of Latin American identities (mestizo, black, indigenous, and others) is increasing.

In the course of the twentieth century modernity entered the bloodstream of the people and their religions. Even though they are excluded and made outcasts, our people in their own way are actors within Latin American mestizo modernity. We have different identities and logics of belief. Therefore, religious inculturation is not restricted to some traditional corners but is found in everyday modernity. However, because modernity dangles goods in front of everyone—though only a few enjoy them—people trust in modernity only conditionally. Hence in the religion of the people there are signs of a relative (not unlimited) adherence to modern civilization. The people are also developing their own alternatives.

Are these practices *syncretist* and/or *inculturated*? The former is a term from the social sciences, while the latter is from theology and pastoral work. I believe that as they act in a number of cultures the people combine things that enable them to survive better and find a sense of complementarity among different elements. Hence, this syncretism of the people does not mix things together for eclectic reasons; it is rather a symbiosis that combines things that serve life. Such syncretism characterizes—or rather, such syncretism is characteristic of—Catholic behavior. Theology pays very little attention to it (and if it does, it is to dismiss it). On the other hand, some church circles see that popular religion is an inculturated way of believing and celebrating. One great expert, Manuel Marzal, explains syncretism as the other side of inculturation, the former being the work of the evangelized and the latter the action of evangelizers.[2] I think this terminology *(syncretism, symbiosis, inculturation)* can help us draw out the sagacious behavior of the Catholic population and of evangelical communities.

Often the traits of popular Christianity come from different cultures and from various religious sources. Several symbol systems are meaningful for one and the same community (and for the people who make it up). In other words, plurality is characteristic not only of our society as a whole but of each component of it (to one degree or another, depending on the history of each group). For example, in the urban religion of ordinary people there are several kinds of inculturation: for illness one goes to a mestizo therapy (and religiosity); in business one assumes the (sacralized) ideology of the market; for one's daily mood one consults the horoscope; to celebrate the life-cycle one requests the sacraments or reads the Word. Thus a single person or a community practices various types of inculturation. Somehow this is all complementary and coherent.

The civilization of progress inculturates a model based on individual and material accomplishments; this myth penetrates into the believing experience of poor, the middle classes, and other sectors, often popularizing dehumanizing powers. Male power is sacralized in the form of keeping women from advancing. Likewise, many attributes of the white elite surround Christian symbols (saints, the Virgin, images of Christ); this is all imbibed uncritically by the Latin American population. In short, there is a good deal of inculturation of sacralized powers. If we wish to be faithful to the incarnate gospel, all of this has to be exculturated.

These issues reach down into deep realities; they are not small details inside the church, nor are they limited to the religious realm. Inculturation—as I insist repeatedly—encompasses the entire human condition.

In addition, there are matters that come from the church realm. In many Christian circles inculturation is mere adaptation and transposition.[3] A single-culture framework is introduced into different situations; the evangelized have to accept and reproduce the world of the evangelizer. Subtly or explicitly, we have here a spiritual and human aggression. On the other hand, some are trying to forge a modern Christian culture (or several of them).[4] They call it inculturation, but their real concern is to rebuild socio-ecclesiastical power within secularized modernity. This project is unworkable. Yet significant sectors are devoted to evangelizing culture, and since the 1980s we are beginning to discover the demands of inculturation.[5]

Thus, in the theoretical debate and especially in the terrain of behavior, there are controversies, and clarifications are needed. These challenges cannot be sidestepped by an inculturation that seeks to be clear-sighted and on the mark, connected to the symbol system and the imagination present in the religions of our peoples.

GUIDEPOSTS FROM HISTORY

Our past and present contain certain noteworthy yet contradictory facts and many-sided processes. This situation cannot be reduced to the church's efforts to deal with religiosity and to evangelize it. We all know that the religious factor encompasses many types of Christian groups, religious systems, sensitivities of faith, and aspects of subjectivity, economics, politics, gender, and much more. Our concern here lies in the everyday agents of inculturation, that is, the believing majorities and their associations (inasmuch as inculturation is not the property of noteworthy figures). Furthermore, we are using a classification that is different from the usual one of colonial times and Christendom, periods of independence, and modernity (that framework comes from those who have led and disfigured the path of Latin American history). Our approach is to evoke inculturation processes of a polycentric character, which both challenge and support the colonial system; we then note how the believing population with its feasts and spiritualities has raised the question of modernization anew, even while it is part of modernity.

Thus, in what follows I interpret the terrain of the Christianities of the people. These are things done by ordinary people. We observe both varieties and creative approaches; many of them indeed have both a primary and a secondary aspect. I take note of what has been done, what is emerging now, and what may happen tomorrow. (No details or scholarly polemics are presented, nor is there any description of the enormous variety of factual situations in our continent.) What I find most striking is that communities of the people have built their Christianities socially and culturally; they contain both degrees of assimilation into the colonial social and religious order and the modern order, and yet there are innovations.

Where does this interpretation spring from? It comes from the "other" and the "other's" history. Popular religion is almost always regarded as particular custom (with no universal value) and as an imperfect and incomplete way of being Christian. This is not helpful for understanding and evaluating it. Rather, one appreciates the inculturation present in the religion of the people when we are alert to the "other" history.[6] Paulo Suess has perceptively questioned the evolutionary vision and the integration or absorption of particular histories into a universal Christianity; the "truth of history" is inseparable from the life project of each people and human group. Twenty years ago Gustavo Gutiérrez made a claim for the "other history . . . in cultural expressions, in popular religion, in the resistance to accepting impositions from the ecclesiastical system," and he cited Leonardo Boff in his critique of what had been written "with a white hand, from those on top." In other words, when we locate ourselves with the "other," that is, in each identity and historic project of the poor, historic landmarks take their own form and do not reproduce official canons.

The basic thrust (which is still operative today) is the variety of ways of feeling, celebrating, and acting with sacred Beings through natural and human mediations. Indeed, it can be said (in current terminology) that for thousands of years our forebears have invented strategies of inculturation—native, Afro-American, Asian, European, mestizo—with their contacts and their boundary lines. Such is not the topic here. Rather, I am going to consider the two great moments; they do not come one after another, nor does one rule out the other. I am then going to point to the lack of communication—and yet some interaction—between church programs and the people's experience of faith, including the issue of exculturation.

POLYCENTRIC AND SYMBIOTIC RELIGIOSITY

The Christianities of the people have forged and recognized many spaces and founts of salvation. This has been done in continuity with the primordial thrust (of the primeval peoples of the continent). During the long period called colonial Christendom, our peoples have developed polycentric and symbiotic universes. The main features are combined with the particular aspects of each human group that calls itself Christian: psychological, pragmatic, mystical, and all the other aspects that are proper to each community and prized by it. I am only going to consider some major features that have sustained believing communities from the colonial period to the present.

In accordance with the features of each region and according to local processes, peoples have developed in their own spaces and times. They have resisted leveling. Persons and groups express their faith at different sites of their own and also in a series of moments in their own calendar that reflects them as a people. This plurality of spaces and of moments of salvific well-being entails a range of religious functions and types of leadership. We also have a number of ways of invoking and understanding the sacred. It looks like a form of polytheism, but actually it is a human polycentrism with its religious reference points. There is room here for diverse interpretations. In studying the beginning of the colonial period in Mexico, Solange Alberro points to "popular and functional polytheism" around shrines and celebrations;[7] such an assessment comes from the philosophy of religion. For myself,

I think it is more proper to talk about believing communities that have constructed their sacred spaces and times.

Various chroniclers, such as Fray Diego Durán, have noted that each human group has its particular relationship with God (in addition to many invocations and celebrations). "In every town, hamlet, and settlement here in New Spain as infidels the Indians had a particular god, and although they had them all and adored them and venerated them and celebrated their feasts, they nevertheless had one in particular whom they pointed to as the advocate of the town . . . as they do now even though they solemnize the feasts of all the saints, nevertheless, they celebrate with full solemnity the feast of the town and of the saint for whom it is named."[8] That is, the sacred place and time were rooted in an advocate, either local or taken from Christendom, according to the identity and history of each community (before and after it became Christian). This is a constant in the way things happen in Latin America. Today the Catholic people maintain different places and moments in the expression of their faith.[9] Many families have an altar and home chapel with a set of images, candles, votive lights, flowers, holy water, charms, and sacred souvenirs. We also have tiny worship centers: grottoes, chapels, crosses, memorials of the dead, public institutions, and private businesses with their sacred corners, and monumental urban and rural shrines. It seems to me that their content is neither worship of false gods nor polytheism. Rather, there is a capacity for reverence and encounter with the Other at significant places and times (without getting caught up in official boundaries). Native growth traditions are rebuilt and to them are added new Christian symbol systems marked by modernity. In short, we have a variety of inculturations, given our intensely religious spaces and times.

A second feature: people combine different things in order to survive and to enjoy the human condition. We can call it a kind of symbiosis. This wisdom has served as the basis for dealing with their basic needs. Within the colonial system, for example, economic servitude has not extinguished the initiatives undertaken by the people (religious associations that proliferate to the point of alarming authorities; artisan shops) but is connected to them. In other words, in the midst of a situation of stratification and marginalization, the people intelligently rebuilt their world and worked with each other while at the same time absorbing things from colonialism. Likewise, they drew on different cultural arrangements to obtain resources and knowledge for survival. This capability of symbiosis has been characteristic of the Christianities of the people.

Why? Has it been due to the people's fuzziness, confusion, and eclecticism? Were they not aware of cultural contradictions? That was not really the reason. Rather, there were wise choices and combinations of those things that were helpful to their life projects. As Eleazar Lopez writes: The people know how "to reformulate their culture . . . in the context of the system," and "they re-read the Christian religion to give continuity within it to the ancestral religious traditions of our peoples."[10] Another understanding of these facts is through the category of *syncretism*. In the first phase of evangelization in Mexico, according to C. Duverger, there was a move from native idolatry to the veneration of the saints, "the factor that opened the door to syncretism."[11] Worship of the saints bolstered indigenous religion. The important thing, in my view, along with conciliation among different religions, is how the outcast reconstructed the Christian tradition. Those who were at a disadvantage vis-à-vis a world that dismissed them have succeeded in combining elements that enriched their way of being Christians.

They faced enormous disadvantages. The powers of the civil, military, and ecclesiastical domains combined to control the mestizo, black, and indigenous populations. They were particularly vigilant over popular religion, into which entered the social order, the economy, colonial morality, and a meaning of life in subjection and with a single center. We may pause to look at public celebrations in the eighteenth century, taking cases from Mexico and Chile.[12]

In the main city in central Mexico, we see the powerful repressed activities of the people at the celebrations of Carnival, Corpus Christi, and All Souls' Day. As J. P. Viqueira indicates, processions, dances, and the placing of candles required the "permission of the church and authorization by the city Council." In 1745, Archbishop Vizarrón closed the church of the Virgin of the Angels because Indians were holding large celebrations around it; that censure lasted for three decades. Colonial authorities worked hand in hand with church bodies, supporting what can be called a monocentric inculturation. Those among the people who internalized this repression can be said to have lived an inculturation of resignation and submission. On the other hand, those among the people who treasured their dignity found their own ways and spaces; they achieved an inculturation of new Christian forms.

Another instance is what happened in Santiago and its rural surroundings in the eighteenth century. Representatives of the church (particularly the leaders of the 1763 synod) worked together with civil and military rulers. Together they made assaults on the ways of life and faith of the common folk. For example, that synod objected to the Mapuche game of the *chueca* and competitions on horseback, and the Captain General immediately forbade such entertainments; the synod decided that shops selling liquor should be open only from 11 A.M. to 1 P.M., and an edict was issued to that effect by the colonial authorities. Indeed, in keeping with the notion that the colonial god stands in opposition to the idols of the Indians, Catholic prelates disapproved of "the sale of food and strong drinks, most of the night being spent in music and dancing; all being prohibited on feasts of the saints; and this being the behavior observed by the gentiles in those of their Idols; so that such gatherings may be called evil; and that is why such gatherings are loathsome to God."[13] The culture-religion of the poor was often called conspiracy, immorality, and idolatry. But the underlying issue is that there were different ways (cultural, political, ethical) of living the Christian faith; there were different inculturations. Unfortunately, this was interpreted by the powerful as a conflict between idols and God.

We also have intercultural relations, in which three major dynamics stand out.

1. On the one hand, we have a vast polycentric universe. Each sector of the people went about building its reality, which differed from others (but without any intention of destroying the others). There was an ability to draw in items from other cultures and to link them with one's own; that is, an inculturation that affirms one's way of being Christian alongside others.

2. On the other hand, there were monocentric positions; that is, a single truth claimed within the framework of Christendom as mediated through the colonial system. This ethnocentrism was not in dialogue with other cultures; it was an inculturation that dismissed others, and put constraints on itself by refusing to meet with the others. The result was ethnocide.[14] According to Barnadas, in Bolivia the church has taken part in ethnocide. Pinto says that missionaries in Chile assumed "an ethnocentric stance and a tendency to ethnocide," although there was a certain amount of tolerance in everyday dealings. This is a harsh judgment based on actual facts; such facts undercut the civilizing intentions of mission activity in colonial times.

3. There were also mestizo Christianities. People traveled in two or more cultural worlds, thereby shaping inculturations that can be called bicultural. Some mixing is unbalanced; that is, the values of the dominant groups hold in subjection and hinder other ways of living. Other mixings are more or less symmetrical; in them the inculturation of the faith manifests an intercultural richness. (What has already been said of the polycentric and symbiotic world of the people goes hand in hand with the mestizo character of the Christianities of common folk.)

Festive and Spiritual Christianity

A second great thrust of history set within Latin American modernity is something that I describe as reaffirmation and innovation in celebration and spirituality. These are the main features of inculturated popular religion. This inculturation gathers momentum because the heart of the people is festive and trusting in sacred, life-giving Beings. These features are bolstered (by way of contrast) when they interact with the kind of constraining pragmatic reason that prevails in our age. It is not simply that the legacies of colonial times are reaffirmed; people are traveling along new paths. It is striking how celebration, when it occurs within modernity, incorporates some modern symbols. Spirituality, for its part, grows in the terrain of the subjective and interpersonal; devotions proper to the modern age arise, and fundamentalisms also spread.

A first trait: the people's Christianity is cheerful. This is a basic feature, not something secondary. The sensitivity, socialization, and mysticism in the faith of the people are all unquestionably festive.[15] There are some misunderstandings about this. Some scholars call the people's religion "ritualistic" (that is true of any religion with its ceremonies), or they under-stand the festive aspect as one part among many. That is not so; it is the very marrow of faith. Among the middle classes and the poor in the city and in the various ethnic traditions, the most characteristic aspect of the faith is its festive ritual character. There are indeed ceremonies that make people sad (in Holy Week, for example), but the common denominator is not a hieratic attitude, but joy, bodily movement, and bodily banqueting, all interwoven with religious activities.

It is well known that there are many worlds of celebration in Latin America and the Caribbean.[16] Here, as in every aspect of the people's religion, we do not have a uniform reality, nor may one speak in the singular about festive inculturation. It is impossible to deal with such worlds in a few paragraphs, so I can only bring out aspects of inculturation.

Modern progress has its secular rituals and also its support from expres-sions of Christianity. A common instance is godfathers and godmothers (in Catholic rites) who have risen socially or belong to a higher stratum, thereby encouraging efforts at upward mobility among the poor and middle sectors with no concern for solidarity. Another instance: at sanctuaries during reli-gious feasts there is a great deal of praying to get rich and the symbols that go along with it (in some Andean shrines people have miniature dollars blessed). We thus have here a faith that is inculturated in obtaining goods and capitalist business dealings.

Another such example is inculturation carried out in rites from birth to death and their commemorations. What is inculturated within family and group cohesion is God's saving presence in rites of passage from one per-sonal situation to another. There is a series of customs around images and their devotions, both large and small; feasts devoted to Mary, Mother of God, and mighty benefactor of believers are especially noteworthy.[17] There is more inculturation here than in worship of Jesus Christ (where ecclesias-tical control tends to be greater). In these multifaceted celebrations we find inculturation spanning a wide range, displaying ethnic, generational, socio-economic, artistic, spiritual, and gender features. This symbolic intensity has made it possible for phenomena from colonial times to pass into the modern age where they are undergoing transformation.

What is happening today? Human beings in modernity are pragmatic and oriented to what is measurable, as opposed to the festive celebration that is joyful and liberated, sharing without selfish calculation. Not only are there contrasts, but these things also tend to be interrelated. Modernity cuts through the festive, and the latter modifies the course of life today. For example, people who are successful economically and politically are those who occupy leading positions, and the community and devout persons are shunted aside; the festive talent of the poor stresses saving for group sharing and regards accumulation of resources for individual benefit as secondary.

This penetration of the modern into the worlds of the people is relatively recent. Certainly modernity has been present in elites in the Americas starting in the sixteenth century as a driving force of modernization. But modernity takes hold only slowly from centers of power, and it fully enters the worlds of the people only in the twentieth century with consolidation of capitalism, modern education, mass media, migration, urban concentrations, and the people's own desire to make progress and to generate their own modern patterns. The Christianities of the people are interacting with modern rationality, subjectivity, and economics with factors of secularization and with the corresponding beliefs and ethics. Who is engaged in such processes? Everyone—and that includes those who are regarded as backward and those who are left out. That is the way modern civilization works; it is planetwide, globalized. In this regard youth play a notable role in modernizing religious celebrations; in such celebrations there is more room for the laity and particularly for young people, who are refashioning the modern world.

A second feature: the Christianity of the people entails an inculturated spirituality. Here (as was also indicated in the previous section) we have behaviors that are solidly rooted in the previous age but also new experiences. Identities and community structures, grassroots and regional movements are gaining strength, women are emerging onto the scene with their associations and programs, political life is in crisis, and ecological and ethic claims are increasing. At the same time, there is some disenchantment with material progress and its absolutes. The pursuit of progress does not fill the human heart. Instead, the sensibilities of the poor who are rooted in the Mystery are budding and flowering.

The believing people clash with the liberal elites. In Peruvian society, for example, "in their campaign for a purer, more rational, and less superstitious faith, the liberals created another intellectual barrier on the road to understanding the popular Catholicism of the Indians and mestizos of the lower class who made up the majority in the country."[18] This problem arises not only with liberals of the classic type; today many social and academic reformers are out of touch with the people. They propose, for example, that the people's religious culture must be purified, on the assumption that it is dehumanized by magic and myth.

Popular groups are deeply spiritual, even though they are continually repressed and discriminated against by the powerful and well educated. There is a need for engaging in discernment out of the people who accept and build life (and not from liberal frameworks or others devised by the elite). Spiritualities bear different signs and inculturated contents. Let us look at some of these matters.

It may seem that the most inculturated spirituality is that of believers with a monolithic identity. Analytically speaking, one can speak of a mestizo, indigenous, or black Christianity; each has its own constants, its imaginaries. But most Latin Americans move about in more than one cultural universe; our Christianities are many-sided and interreligious. Both everyday behavior and spirituality are heterogeneous. In the case of the Andean peoples, for example, their mystical relationship with Mother Earth continues while at the same time the migratory and urban multitudes regard money as the source of existence. It seems to me that discernment can examine the accents in believing action (I next take up three types of spirituality), and then see the overall orientation of spirituality.

I see three types of inculturated spirituality.

Type A: devotional alliance. The traditional version is direct and ongoing contact with a (male or female) saint to whom one prays and whom one celebrates. It may be the patron saint of a town, the object of an association of devotees, or a mass shrine. Another version of devotional alliance is more individual and familiar: around the Sacred Heart, the Virgin of Lourdes or Fatima, devotions promoted by religious congregations, the Legion of Mary, and so forth. Each of these "alliances" has its history and specific meaning. A common factor is interaction between believers and a Protector. It is a mystical interaction with concrete implications in health, solving family and economic problems, and many more things.

Type B: militant spirituality. This is the spirituality of groups and modes of expression chosen by each person, where one is a member and carries out particular customs. The following spiritualities stand out: sacramental (active members of a church or parish group), biblical (new Catholic experiences, evangelical communities, biblically oriented catechetical programs), and social (branches of Catholic Action, and new social and religious groups). Inculturation here entails the modern subject who takes initiatives and joins with others for self-improvement and to strengthen the presence of the church in the world today.

Type C: occasional spirituality. Many Catholics participate sporadically and selectively in church activity and in modalities of popular worship, for example, prayer at grave sites and memorials to the dead, attachment to amulets, rituals for protecting oneself against evil and bad luck, ceremonies in emergency situations. I am struck by the number of initiatives among the middle classes (in the Peruvian highlands) with their images, pyramids and crystals, rituals with vegetables like the rue, attachment to figures like the Buddha or the recent "mushroom from India," or the dried toad. Generally they are seeking personal success and fortune. This seems to me to be a kind of informal and religiously plural inculturation, carried out by people who have a gift for syncretism. Many say they are Catholic, but they shape the Christian imaginary in their own way, introducing elements from other religious worlds.

These three types of inculturation tend to have contacts with one another (particularly type A with type C). They differ from one another, but they tend not to be exclusive (except in some cases of type B). Certainly other modes of spirituality exist. My concern here is in the differing and partly complementary inculturations that the people fashion in living out their faith.

What then are the overall directions? I consider three thrusts: relationality, modern beliefs (fundamentalism, consumption of the religious, history-making ethics), and sacralization of the material. We have already considered some accretions in action (types A, B, and C). I now turn to something more comprehensive: human contact with the sacred. I am not going to consider the content but rather the orientation, the directionality of modern popular spirituality.

A first spiritual consideration is its relational character. Starting from basic human needs, the Christian people have an intense faith relationship with symbols of life. This is a spirituality incarnate in the pursuit of bread and everyday health, in love, in ways of dealing with fear and conflict, in ties to the dead. In the midst of situations of vulnerability and uncertainty, people within the poor and the marginal communities establish spiritual relationships that are connected to humane alternatives.

A second trait is beliefs marked by modernity. This is the case of fundamentalisms; they seem to be opposed to the contemporary spirit, but deep down they are ways of adjusting to contexts of modernity. Fundamentalism concentrates on one thing—the Bible, a Catholic image, a ritual system—and so one can get by in today's world without questioning it. Some Catholic and evangelical circles exalt certain sacred realities and ignore social change. These are dualistic stances that are partly a challenge to an inhumane order; they can easily be manipulated by the powerful. Another variant of modernity is to be a consumer of the religious. Each individual chooses what he or she feels is necessary. As Imelda Vega Centeno observes, Catholics consume "goods of salvation within the broad and heterodox religious market today: The result is a syncretic religious practice . . . without entering into contradiction with the official religion they say they profess nor with the modernity of their ways of life."[19] Another modality is to place the accent on ethics within history. Christianity is lived, not so much in an ecclesial manner, but especially as well-being and justice with oneself and others. Pragmatic and pluralistic values proper to the secularized world are also cultivated. In short, these three ways of believing (fundamentalistic, consumption of religion, humanistic ethics) are inculturations that are in tune with the spirit of modernity.

A third thrust is sacralizing material things. This would seem not to form part of the spiritual, yet Christians plainly absolutize material success. Sometimes it is more the orientation of a desire to be rich, inasmuch as the overwhelming reality is that most people live on the edge. This is a materialist mystique supported by Christian formulas and symbols: "God gives to the early riser," that is, to one who wins economically. The saints are often invoked for business and getting rich.

In short, the guideposts of contemporary inculturation are the festive and the spiritual (with its variety of forms) that enable poor peoples to survive and transcend their daily wants.

The people's religious forms partially assimilate the patterns of modernity: subjectivity, reason, technologies, and the globalized economic and cultural order. We observe dynamics of exclusion and cooptation. Yet there is resistance and spaces and moments that are alternatives to the unjust order. There are Christian inculturations that reproduce modern dehumanization; there are inculturations of relations that generate life. To understand which is which we need only examine their basic orientations.

When we rigorously examine the condition of modernity, we can see that its crisis is structural and that it is trapped. The philosopher H. de Lima Vaz sums it up in these words: "A crisis of the subject seeks to be the center of reference of everything that reason can say of the real."[20] In this regard I have emphasized inculturations in the religion of the people that give priority to relationships between subjects and with the sacred (and not to the individual in himself or herself). Religious symbols are reasonable, but they are not enclosed in the dominant logic. It can therefore be said that the deep crisis of modern civilization has been faced and to some extent resolved through the inculturated religious forms of the people. These are the vectors of popular religion (not all of it), that of the people who believe in and build life in a relational, festive, and mystical manner.

INTERACTIONS IN THE RELIGIOUS FIELD

We now go on to look at inculturation in the midst of the successes and missteps and the tensions and correlations that take place in the religious field. An either-or approach does not fit our situation: *the* church (its public representatives) officially handling inculturation *vs. the* religion of the people engaging in an inculturation of lesser value. Both subjects are multiple in shape, heterogeneous, distant from one another but linked. Inculturation has many authors (not just two), with their successes and missteps. I am going to consider four dimensions in the religious field: violence, symbol systems, ethics, and absolutization. For methodological purposes, I prefer to focus on these crucial dimensions in each age rather that limiting myself to the historical sequence of the church (Latin American Christendom from the sixteenth century onward, neo-Christendom and modern reforms, and the conciliar period with its advances and retreats). Moreover, in the properly ecclesial terrain there is systematic failure to communicate, because of different strategies. The leadership of the church is concerned about teaching and leading the people; the latter, for their part, are concerned about human needs confronted with faith. As Imelda Vega Centeno says, "What institutional religions offer is basically ideological, while what the bulk of the population demands is related to very concrete basic needs."[21] These discordant orientations lead to different ways of correlating faith and culture.

A first point: the culture of aggression/fear with which peoples have been made Christian. In the religious structures of the people there are deep imprints of social and spiritual violence; people have internalized fear. The dominant groups (where many ecclesiastics are situated) view popular religion with colonial eyes (it is the realm of the devil) or with the eyes of modernity (it is the world of ignorance and superstition).

I pause to consider some landmarks.[22] The main events involving bishops in the New World have an aggressive thrust to them. The Third Council of Lima (1582-83) described the beings who protect the natives: "They are not gods but rather devils." The Third Council of Mexico (1585) proposed evangelization "so that they may not walk in the hands of the devil." Clear-eyed pastoralists, like Bernardino de Sahagún and the famous twelve Franciscans in Mexico, also assume that these gods are devils who deceive the indigenous and make them practice idolatry. Moving on to reforms in modernity, the Brazilian bishops in 1915 (in an action that left its stamp on this great church until Vatican II) made parish control binding over celebrations and rites in marginal chapels (and added, "police authority will help"), ordered the teaching of the faith by the church (outside the church there is no salvation), and emphasized that besides teaching there must be sacraments. A few years previously the Council of Bishops of Latin America (1899) declared, "The effective remedy for superstition is the knowledge and profession of the Catholic faith which dispels ignorance."

These are quite categorical stances. The devils are replaced by God through the use of violence. People have two options: being saved (receiving the church's teaching and keeping the commandments) or suffering eternal damnation (if they continue with idolatrous practices and superstitions). Such inculturations are colonialist and rationalist in nature. On the side of the people faith is misrepresented by the culture of submission and faith. The most serious thing is that the lowly disqualify themselves when they regard themselves as possessed by the devil (colonization) or by ignorance (modernity).

A second point: symbol systems. Catholic pastoral activity and evangelical action engage in a rich inculturation to the extent that such activity is rich in symbols. Churches are spaces full of symbols of salvation, which are accepted and reinterpreted by ordinary people. We Catholics in particular offer images, sacraments, and feast days; for their part, the Evangelicals spread the Word, healing, and community. These things enter into people's everyday life, where they are rebuilt and given a new direction as a result of the people's capacity for inculturation.

Catholic evangelization and its assimilation by sectors of the people affirm the cosmic side of things, the ethic of life, celebration, and ritual. Women provide leadership for a great deal of these beliefs and activities; they are much more alert to the symbolic and provide a great deal of inculturating leadership. Mestizo, Afro-American, and indigenous peoples are sagaciously regenerating signs of life out of their own roots. In this sense Catholicism has provided room for marginalized individuals and peoples who are building their own versions of Catholic faith. Such achievements are acknowledged by non-confessional scholars. Peter Berger, for example, sees "in Catholicism . . . the presence incorporated into the modern world of some of the most ancient religious aspirations of the human being."[23] I will return to this matter in the next theological section.

In evangelical churches, saving faith goes hand in hand with solidarity between brothers and sisters in the faith; today there are also flourishing social and political expressions of living in Christ; inculturation is also evident in healing and in being community. Yet there is talk of a break with the "world" (which entails distance from cultural traits); faith is exalted and works are downplayed; and leaders tend to be authoritarian. In other words, there are aspects that seem to run against inculturation from below. With regard to healing, along with prayers to Christ and to the Spirit, human action is extremely important: imposition of hands, consolation, advice, and much more.[24] Obviously there are ambiguous things in these Christian spaces, but they are inculturated.

A third point: ethics. In the behavior of the people we find codes, norms, and fundamental options that make up part of a "culture of life." Law is important insofar as it makes possible living more fully and better. But this is being harnessed to some extent by modern individualism. In his study of Brazil, Pedro Ribeiro de Oliveira shows that since the turn of the century the doctrine of salvation and the use of sacraments and devotions have served the privatization of faith and ethics.[25] The communitarian is not annulled, but the responsibility and freedom of each believer to do good or evil is highlighted. Something similar can be seen in other situations. In the urban context examined by Juan C. Cortázar, university students maintain the basically sacral and protective view of the people's religiosity, but it is not "the independent activity of the subject" that comes to the fore.[26] In general, one finds that ethical individualism is fueled by the contemporary cultural setting and by church activity. Fortunately, it is filtered through family and community traditions, where the inculturation of the morality of the common good is cultivated.

A fourth point: absolutization of human things. I am referring to absolutizations that abuse the "other"; one type of rationality is sacralized and other logics are dismissed; certain rites are judged to be the only saving signs, and other symbol systems are classified as pagan and magic. These and other absolutizations have features that in theological language are called idolatry. What is called for is exculturation; that is, idolatrous expressions have to be separated from the Christian expressions. Who carries out this task? Exculturation, like inculturation, is a mission of each ecclesial community.

Several human processes in Latin America are helpful for critical exculturation. Vast numbers of migrants are rebuilding their ways of life in the cities. Young people tend to be multicultural, and they spur social innovations and relativize the unchangeable. Organizations of the people aware of their rights and opposed to structural marginalization also tend to question dehumanizing religious factors. Women continue to establish relations of reciprocity, thereby challenging the patriarchal norm, among other things. Hence from several angles what is regarded as sacred is being relativized and new paradigms are being generated. Conditions are propitious for exculturation.

It is an ecclesial task to be concerned about representations of God. Our mestizo peoples are discovering the faces of God, and they are not tied to a white Nordic image of divinity. In ethics and spirituality Christian patterns linked to power and its idols are being questioned, and the law of treating others well, of unconditional love, is being reaffirmed. Also exculturated is the primacy given to individual pleasure in order to celebrate faith in a way that persons and communities may have full communion with God.

Also to be faced is the economic-religious realm, namely, the idol of money. Few go so far as to love only capital, but it is very common to connect it to the sacred. This connection is growing, and it affects the meaning of the economy as a necessary and humanizing means (and not as end and measurement of everything). Increasingly persons, events, and religious things are measured with the yardstick of monetary yield. We are told that these are the laws of a society that is moving forward, but actually these are idolatrous dynamics. Franz Hinkelammert says it quite clearly: "The divinization of the market creates a money-God: 'in God we trust.'"[27] This modern dogma makes its way into the sensitivity and understanding of the faith. In my area of the Andes, for example, there is widespread use of a certain "decoration" for home and workplace: a tiny image of Christ or Mary surrounded by a great amount of paper currency, primarily American. This money-god must without a doubt be exculturated.

Accordingly, several types of inculturation are interacting in the religious field. Some tend to be monocentric (for example, the absolutizing of money); they call for exculturation. Others tend to be polycentric and display the creativity of different human sectors that wager on life. I have emphasized the challenge of exculturating the worship of money, which polarizes people and blocks communication—and most of all disfigures the presence of God.

THEOLOGICAL FACETS

Together with the phenomenological and historical approaches to understanding the religion of the poor, it is also important to also pursue the theological approach. This route brings us into the entire being and acting of the people (and does not keep us solely on the level of beliefs and rituals).

First, it is a matter of reading salvation history. The hermeneutical principle is that God's saving designs are revealed to each person and people. Each person and human community responds or does not respond to God's love, and these responses have their ethical, political, cultural, religious, and other mediations. With regard to our topic—inculturations in the religion of the poor—the relationship between religion and theology should be clarified. I do not agree with the standard often used, which sees the religiosity of Latin American people as something human that serves as preparation for revelation (something like an "old testament") and Christian life as that which allows for doing theology of the true God. A different vision has been proposed in our continent: a salvation history, of which the church is sacrament, becomes present in every human journey and spirituality of our peoples. Without this vision one is (humanly) ethnocentric and (theologically) ecclesiocentric.

Just what is this reading? Many make it in a linear and evolutionary manner, and so modernity means that everything earlier has been surpassed. For example, stress is placed on the relationship between a believing subject and his or her God. Or stages are traced from Jewish beginnings to final revelation to the apostles. Our methodological option throughout this work is to draw the history of faith (and theology) out of the common people, namely, from the Christianities that actually exist in Latin America, where inculturation has taken place and continues. In a general sense what is at stake is the historicity of faith and its inculturations. As W. Beinert points out, in the history of the human being "truth can be approached continually."[28]

Inculturation is now beginning to make its way into the terrains of theological work. Its antecedents are the many contributions on the evangelization of culture that were ratified by the documents of Vatican II. With regard to inculturation, one observes the many-sided modality of living the Christian event in the church thanks to the work of the Spirit. What stands out in that many-sidedness are the religious paths taken by the poor. They have, as Cristián Parker says, "another logic," which is displayed particularly in the religion of the people, which brings with it a thrust toward humanization.[29] The bearer of inculturation is each concrete community of faith, with its own "other logic," with its believing wisdom.

People are beginning to follow out these leads in Catholic settings. Inculturation has been given a clear impetus by the bishops at the Fourth Conference of Latin American and Caribbean Bishops (in Santo Domingo). Some theologians are now beginning to connect inculturation to the religion of the people.[30] From a conservative standpoint in Mexico, Javier Lozano says, "Popular religiosity . . . at its core is the inculturation of the faith in the deep cultural values of the people." With its vision "from below" the Bolivian episcopate supports oppressed cultures in the struggle for dignity and commits itself to "accompany popular religiosity in a trusting and critical way so that it may come to be a privileged expression of the inculturation of Catholic faith and may lead to a commitment of faith and life." In Brazil, Alberto Antoniazzi makes realistic proposals. He notes how inculturation has advanced in indigenous and black settings; he asks whether steps taken in base communities are toward inculturation or toward modernization; and he notes that there is little inculturation in urban settings and in modernity. I believe that promising approaches are opening up and good questions are being asked.

Next I take note of some theological facets. In examining the faith of the
ordinary folk we see clear signs that Christian existence has been inculturated:
their community faith, ethical priority placed on the neighbor, a relational
approach especially by women, prayer and following of Christ and Mary,
and much more. I am now going to take up some aspects that seem obscure,
where inculturation seems to be most difficult: the cosmic side of popular
religion, healing, celebration, and wisdom. In speaking about these matters,
let us not forget that the theological is not reduced to the strictly religious,
because we assess and value theologically the Christian journey, the history
of each people. As Paulo Suess states well, "This history of the other is the
ordinary path to salvation."[31] Accordingly, we are drawing out of the history of each community the presence of the God who is Savior of all
humankind.

The cosmic facet is very much alive in Latin America and the Caribbean,
particularly in indigenous and Afro-American inculturation and in mixed
races. It is partly because of these cultural roots that Catholicism is intensely cosmic; for example, the use of water, fire, and vegetables in all
kinds of domestic and public prayers; religious community with the earth
(especially in birth and death); ongoing interaction with those who have
died; cyclical rites; and many sites that have a sacred significance. In general, there is a sacred relationship between humankind and the surrounding
living and inanimate beings; there is a close relationship between bodiliness
and spiritual energy. These things are being questioned and modified, however, because of contemporary Christian anthropocentrism influenced by
modernity's concentration on self.

Latin American Christianity is enriched by the cosmic and ecological
aspects contributed by popular religion. Inculturation accordingly touches
further dimensions; the bodily and the spiritual are reunited. Salvation history includes (and does not turn away from) the cosmic context. There is a
rediscovery of how all things have been created in Christ and are held together in him (see Col 1:16-17). Evangelization becomes "eco-inculturated."

Healing is another basic facet in a theology that is sensitive to the
inculturation practiced in the religion of the people. Much of the activity of
believers has to do with handling illnesses and pain, with recovering emotional, bodily, communal, and mystical equilibrium. As in the previous point,
the mestizo, black, Amerindian and other cultural sources are decisive. They
serve as the basis for a rereading of the Word of God, and especially the
healing action of Jesus. The Lord proclaimed the reign and healed sick people
(see Mt 4:23). This is attested by the experience and theology of grassroots
Catholics and Evangelicals. I stress the Catholic side, because it is often
thought that Evangelicals are the only ones who engage in healing. A great
deal of the supportive prayer and activity of Catholics is related to healing.
In calling upon God, Christ and the saints are seen as those who assure
health. In the eyes (the theological intuition) of the poor, Christian salvation means going from illness to well-being.

The facet of celebration is also extremely important. It can be said that it is the greatest mediation of the people's faith-hope-love. It is a sacramental mediation and an inculturated time-and-space. It is how the people experience the Pasch, and how they (unthematically) grasp the Resurrection. Yet celebration by Catholics is extremely ambivalent and complex. There are oppressive and escapist structures, experiences of evil (such as racial and social discrimination), and the sin of violence. In the midst of all this is the inculturated experience of God, allied with the community celebrating its faith (through the patron saint, for example). God is known and adored as the source of joy. In ethical terms, celebration encourages hope for a life without abusive treatment, and it makes joy and communion goals of human activity. The ethics of the gospel, expressed in the beatitudes (Mt 5:4-5), comes from a God who gives joy to those who mourn and gives the earth to the humble; this takes place in authentic celebrations.

A fourth theological facet of inculturation found in the religion of the poor is wisdom. Faith communities make their theology explicit through the narrative, the symbolic, the artistic, and the ethical. This is a believing wisdom in accordance with a relational model of living history. It is also a multicultural wisdom that combines various religious traditions. Another important aspect is the discernment of the modern. Not long ago an Aymara neighbor said to me, "Science moves forward and that's fine, but I ask, 'Why does it move forward?'" What she meant was that progress is less important than nondiscriminatory humanization. On the other hand, however, we have the weight of a dichotomous reason (true/false, good/bad, more civilized/more backward) and religious intolerance (increased by various phenomena of fundamentalism).

I want to emphasize the quality of knowledge of God. This happens even though colonial Christendom set God over against native beliefs, which reject it as demonic. But the *sensus fidei* has gone beyond this and other false either/ors. In commenting on the Incarnation, Sor Juana Ines de la Cruz, the most important theologian of the colonial period, considering the text of Deuteronomy 4:7, says: "What nation is so great that it enjoys gods so familiar as our God does with us? . . . O mystery of the Incarnation . . . wedding of the Only-begotten with human nature!"[32] She does not seem to place the native deities and God at odds. The approach to the Mystery has the depth of familiarity (as Sor Juana Inés says). A constant in the experience of inculturated faith in our continent is tolerance toward the various ways of calling on the holy. Divinity cannot be boxed up or used to disqualify cultures different from one's own.

By way of conclusion, I highlight the points made in this chapter and some of the convictions that underlie my presentation.

The Christianities of the people have carried out different and profound inculturations. I think that they are solid foundations out of which church bodies can work together on inculturation. They are plural and polycentric, and they have a symbolic and festive quality. I have also emphasized the agents and fruits of inculturation throughout the history of peoples and communities with their identities and life projects. In short, inculturation encompasses all dimensions of reality.[33] Yet the (inculturated?) Christian supports for discriminatory power and for racist and anthrocentric stances have to be removed, together with the supports that privatize faith and at the same time sacralize the capitalist order.

I have certain convictions. For reasons of the heart, and for a social option in tune with the gospel, for some years I have been discovering "from within" both wonderful things and distortions in popular religion. I make a distinction between things that are humanizing and factors adverse to the welfare of the people. More deeply, one sees the revelation of God and the salvation history that calls to each people. Yet as a teacher and a priest (who has not been born or educated with the faith of simple people) I have a vision "from outside." That is valuable but secondary; the main thing is living experience from within of the people's spirituality and praxis.

It seems to me that the great challenge today is to shape ways for people to be happy and in solidarity by getting beyond those places where modernity is stuck. To put it in positive terms, civilizations are back on the drawing board. They emerge out of poor communities, out of peoples who suffer and are visionary, out of women with their relational and transforming perspective, out of the energies of young people who are exploring uncharted paths. In the Christianities of the people, in their religious inculturations, there are many signs of these new shapes.

6

Andean Religious Life

As male and female members of religious orders with Andean fates and hearts, we have been involved in church renewal for the past several decades. The gospel option for the poor and for their life-giving cultures demands that we be inculturated.

Throughout Latin America religious life is in a period of change, for several reasons. Here are the aspects that I regard as most important.

1. The liberation approach, which arouses feelings and controversy, entails a rethinking of religious life. It means getting distance from the powers of this world and placing ourselves at the service of a new humankind; it reaffirms the vocation to the Reign and the liberating work of Jesus and his disciples.

2. The biblical renewal—especially the reading of the Word from the margins and from a gender perspective—challenges and energizes religious life; it is nourished by prayerful reading done by the people of God, a reading with the eyes of women and the eyes of men who prize mutuality.

3. The rediscovery of the particular history and charism of each congregation and religious order. Some international orders and congregations value their involvement and reestablishment in our continent.

4. A beautiful journey, thanks to processes of personal prayer and community retreat, where we are moved by the love of God, and where Christ calls us to a radical discipleship today and tomorrow.

5. The martyrdom of men and women religious alongside so many others in the Latin American church; this blood is fruitful and pulls us out of routine and brings us into closer association with the Crucified One.

6. The ways of being involved in suffering and struggle for a better world, which includes inculturation and interculturality. I am going to highlight this last dimension. I note general aspects and use the Andes, where I do my own work, by way of example.

In considering the sociocultural realm, one is led to appreciate human roots and designs in the complex world of the ordinary people. But in the so-called popular cultures, we find subordination and alienation, along with resistance, creativity, and interaction with other worlds. The overall setting is modernity, whose own crisis is that of a change of era. Such are the contexts in which inculturation and the relationship between cultural processes are unfolding. With regard to our topic here, the question emerges: Are these things re-creating religious life? How is witness of the reign of God changing? It seems to me that religious life is being solidly refashioned within the journey of the poor and believing people. Religious life is in turn contributing to the life projects and fidelity to the Spirit to which the entire people of God is called.

My observations here are presented in three stages. I first review the challenges presented to us by the context of modernity. I then examine the neologism *inculturation* and its impact on religious life. Then I consider the charismatic aspect in Andean religious life. This is all a way of reworking the preferential option for the poor that has revolutionized the Latin American church in all its expressions.

THE CONTEXT OF MODERNITY AND ITS CHALLENGES

In every corner of today's world, society and culture are marked by globalized modernity. Any proposal for inculturation must take this into account. To do otherwise is to take refuge in unreality. Thus, it is amusing when those in some religious houses say they are rescuing culture with some piece of folk art. Actually, the great challenge today is to continue to build religious life that is modern and inculturated.[1]

As a preliminary point, over the years I have noted a change of language in environments of renewal, including those of religious life. People have gone from saying, "I think that . . . " to "I feel that . . . " These are not simply words; such language expresses cultural shifts. The first expression is rational and strictly modern; the second expression has a postmodern tinge where the accent is placed on enjoying the present. It used to be that one blindly sought to fulfill the objectives of religious life. In the modern way of life things are thought about and questioned. And now postmodern sensitivity is spreading, where there are no standards and each individual claims his or her own authenticity.

It is well to review the modern and its challenges. We can all see that modernity has certain main lines: rationality, freedom, subjectivity, autonomy, critical vision. It is worthwhile to evaluate what has been received, question the established order, organize democracy, and raise the question of transforming reality as a whole. This is already a driving force in many religious congregations; it is likewise the framework for any proposal for inculturation. On the other hand, we see that in our societies modernity also leads to inequality, impoverishment, deceitful idols, and devaluation of cultures. What are the challenges we face? First, modernity has to be subjected to discernment, along with its universal accomplishments, its deceptions and dehumanizations, and its potentialities. It is also obvious that modernity has enriched religious life; for example, personal abilities are recognized; there is an accent on community and intimacy; the church (including religious) serves renewal of the contemporary world; modern means are used in the apostolate; value is placed on dialogue, pluralism, and democratic shared responsibility. I think that what is most important in putting modern values in religious life is how doing so deepens and enhances the lives of the people in poverty whom we serve. The goal sought in faith-inspired action and witness is not modernity but rather the life of all people.

I am going to venture some comments on the postmodern. I see that certain features of modernity are being dethroned: reason that supposedly explains reality, an all-powerful technology, and illusory plans for progress. Yet postmodernism upholds skepticism, inaction, hedonism, and it exalts the present moment devoid of any ethics, any history, or any utopia. With regard to religious life, the postmodern has both lights and shadows. It is well to give a new value to sensibility, the festive, and the symbolic—and to nuance the rational. At the same time, it is somewhat superficial and one-sided to give priority to feeling by separating off other vital dimensions such as morality and action in history. Our vocation as Christian persons is not simply individual satisfaction, but that which makes us free to love responsibly.

In the contemporary world each people is facing such realities, which are also the setting for religious life and its striving for inculturation. But modernity is an overarching civilization. It has many specific modalities; inculturation is carried out in each of them.[2] Let us look at this modern set of issues in the world of the Andes and then at the charism of being religious.

ANDEAN INCULTURATION

The Andean way of life has been forged over the course of over ten thousand years, and it has been changing rapidly in the last few decades. The behaviors and identities of Andeans and their communities are emerging.

I begin by noting two disturbing facts about religious life: the disincarnate way we speak about God, and the way we describe ourselves.

God is said to be present in the Amerindian peoples. That statement implies that in our prayers and proclamation we visualize God with Andean features, and yet that is generally not done. Representations of God do not have Andean colors, flavors, melodies, and spiritualities. References to God are still chained to images chosen by small groups of colonizers. Neither in joint pastoral work nor in religious life is God often seen to be taking on flesh and paschal mystery in Andean things. (Something similar may be said about Afro-American, mestizo, rural, and urban settings.)

Certain stereotypes are in effect: God is presented as one of the white race, bearing the signs of power of wealthy minority groups. These ideas come from schooling and from the European type of religiosity that has spread everywhere. We have done very little inculturation of prayer and celebration, proclamation and catechesis. The fact that God is not identified in an incarnate, paschal, and pentecostal way to me seems to correlate with the fact that we do not as Christians (and in our case as female and male religious) embrace the rich paschal and spirit-filled realities of each Latin American person and community.

Moreover, I find it regrettable that we generally present ourselves (and are described by others) with categories that are partial and not inculturated. What is highlighted is each person's first and last name, the name of the congregation or religious order, address, nationality, professional status, and responsibility in terms of power. When we are classified in this manner, we enroll in the dominant social and religious order; in other words, we inculturate ourselves in certain spaces of power. Another approach is to recognize and value what is one's own on both a small and large scale; that is, to be identified as Andean (and, for example, from the community of Paucarcolla) and as part of the Peruvian nation; as Quechua or Aymara or mestizo; as part of the poor portion of humankind; as a devotee of such-and-such a saint of our birthplace; as a person within the process of social and cultural change. Why does all of this tend to be concealed? These are issues of identity, and there is a spiritual vacuum as well.

These and other everyday facts indicate the problematic nature and urgency of this issue. It is well to ask ourselves about the what and who, and then consider church activity and religious identity in terms of the correlation between faith and cultures.

WHAT? WHO? HOW?

Let us look at the nature and subjects of inculturation.[3] In the Andean setting where the people have received Christianity and re-created it, they have carried out their own inculturation processes. Christian faith has entered into the symbolic universe and Andean praxis. What then is inculturation? It is the Andean way of living Christian faith in a way that is incarnate, paschal, and spirit-filled. Who is doing it? The wide range of identities and associations that have been formed and are being transformed here in the Andes. Broadly speaking, the Andean church is the subject of inculturation. Therefore, as men and women religious we can join its ranks and make a contribution to what has already been done by way of inculturation in each Andean community. This is a charismatic presence at the heart of such processes; we are not in charge, nor are we the authors of such processes.

Yet this Andean reality is marked by what happens around the world. This can be characterized in a number of ways. A basic issue is what has been called the crisis of civilization. It is not that there is a crisis in one country or another, but rather all modern civilization seems to be undergoing a radical crisis. It is true that this civilization has succeeded in penetrating the entire planet, and all peoples, and that it has energized each local and regional culture. However, it also has seemingly insuperable limitations, in particular the destructive force of nuclear energy, the genetic crisis, and the issue of ecology. Conditions are being created for new civilizations to develop. Their outlines are not yet defined, and indeed they seem to be still in gestation. (I am not here talking about so-called postmodernity, which reflects a dissidence within modernity.)

In our own setting, alongside a peculiarly Andean modernity, we detect some seeds of new human conditions. On all sides—and that includes these Andean regions—we have emerging and previously inexperienced situations. They do not yet constitute something distinct from and opposed to modern civilization, but they are germs of hope. Here are a few of their elements: ways of consensus and organization in the everyday setting (given the collapse of the overarching system of political representation); fruitful small-scale economic initiatives; very precise ecological proposals in each particular place; affirmation of women, and from both women and men a reconstruction of social fabrics; folk art, which is spreading an alternative imaginary; youth organizations; repudiation of the idolatry of the market; persistence and reorganization of Andean spirituality and ethics.

These elements are like a river carrying the waters of the inculturation of the Good News of Jesus Christ and upon which inculturated religious life is being refashioned. It has already been said that the subjects are the modern Andean communities (with their Quechua, Aymara, and mestizo identities) in the city and rural areas; these communities are giving rise to new ways of being human. Religious life contributes to these processes, even as it assumes and questions them. We take our place both on the terrain of the particular Andean modernity and in the emerging cultural forms.

We exculturate and inculturate ourselves. On the one hand, we face uncritical acceptance of modern neo-colonialism through the media, the school system, advertising, and secular entertainment. Occasionally these may include some pseudo-Christian ingredients—the fact that a few "get ahead" is attributed to divine providence, or me-first and "good feeling" in disregard of others is given religious legitimation. We should exculturate ourselves from this dominant order, which is an assault on the gospel of Life. Out of the gospel we confront the contemporary idols that manipulate what is Christian.

And yet, we do inculturate ourselves. This takes place within the emerging processes and identities. In this regard I want to emphasize a series of forms of mestizo identity, the increasing preponderance of youth in Andean identity, and symbolic creativity.

Taking up mestizaje first, we are all aware of its ambivalences. In one sense, such mixing re-creates cultural inheritances, those with indigenous roots interacting with new constructions of Andean identity; yet mestizaje is imitative and copies dominant patterns. These ambiguities can be seen in Andean Christianity, which is basically mestizo. In the specific case of religious life we may ask which mestizo forms it takes on and which it does not.

Another major phenomenon is the youthful profile of the Andean world, where for centuries older people decided everything. Youth is today the main driving force, and not only numerically. Its leadership is mestizo and innovative. For example, in the highlands many young people devote hours and hours to playing the traditional *zampoña* (bamboo flute) and dancing in their own manner, yet at the same time they are training themselves in technology, science, and computers. Young people, in other words, are combining cultural elements and opening new paths. They are the protagonists of inculturation (and thus they are not tied to the customs of their ancestors). In religious life, new members from among them can move the inculturation process forward.

We also have the driving force of the Andean symbolic universe. Some symbolic forms are losing esteem, others are undergoing change, and some new buds are springing forth. Migrants in cities, and in general that portion of the Andean population that is in contact with other ways of life, obviously are the ones changing Andean symbol systems. Thus, the task of inculturation:

- is carried out with established symbols, such as Mother Earth, ties with dead people, and Andean associations; and
- is very alert to emerging symbols, such as urban languages, rituals for good luck, transitory community organizations, and new ways of sensing and representing God. The identities of religious men and women unfold in the midst of these processes (mestizaje, increasing role of youth, elaboration of symbols, as well as others). Such identities are not static; our "we" combines past, present, and future.

We religious men and women are located as Christians within such processes, and yet we have our own charism. We are not impartial judges or observers, but we ourselves are actors, alongside many other people. All of us as persons are called to give witness to the reign of God and to live in the Spirit. We are present with the charism proper to the profession of religious life, which has its prophetic dimension and its inculturated character. Thus, the human advance toward freedom makes an absolutely essential contribution. As CLAR spokespersons have said, the prophetic charism entails questioning "all human and church structures insofar as they are embodiments of still-unfolding history and not yet the definitive shape of the Reign."[4] In combination with what is contributed by others, our charism helps purify and redirect church mission in today's world. We are also present with an inculturating drive, which is from the Spirit. In short, as service to the reign, the vowed life accents the prophetic, and as fidelity to the Spirit, it stresses inculturation.

CHURCH STRATEGIES

It is well to recall that Vatican II discussed the evangelization of culture (in the singular) and that its statements were carried further by Paul VI in *Evangelii Nuntiandi* and by the conference of Latin American bishops at Puebla (now in the plural: evangelization of cultures). In 1992 the Santo Domingo conference devoted forty-one paragraphs to inculturation. This church option is advancing in several directions. I think there are three main strategies, and that religious life is unfolding in each of them.

A first strategy is that of each community engaged in inculturation. This represents a long journey. For centuries the primordial people, as well as Afro-American and mestizo sectors, urban sectors, middle classes, and elites have been accepting Christian faith, in accordance with the identities and cultural projects of each. One can also recognize the inculturation capability that is present throughout popular Catholicism, base Christian communities, apostolic movements, and many other places. As the Santo Domingo document states (SD 55, 230, 243, 248-50), these processes are taking place within the community and the particular church, and their goal is liberation. In general, I think Latin American religious life has had very little presence in these inculturating currents of the people (rather, it has become comfortable in middle-class and elite circles). Hence, a great challenge for us is to become established as religious communities in the midst of the range of identities of Latin American people and their innovating inculturation.

A second strategy is that of building Christian cultures. Some propose that it be in the singular: mestizo-Christian culture. This is not feasible if we consider the heterogeneity of peoples, modern secularization, and the fact that particular identities are being reaffirmed. Even so, a great deal of church action is moving forward implicitly or explicitly, with this neo-Christendom thrust. We observe that many educational programs, social action, and certain types of catechesis and liturgy, promote "properly Christian cultural values." To some extent, this stance was taken up in the text of Santo Domingo (SD 13, 24, 27, 31, 33, 45, 97, 229, 263), but not as its primary option. It seems to me that many apostolic institutions and ways of life as religious men and women are located in this strategy of a "Christian culture." Apostolic works favor the formation of modern citizens with a Christian mindset; rarely do they strive for alternatives that would be more human. What stands out in the internal life of religious congregations is its uniformity with a seemingly supra-cultural common denominator. The upshot is that the different identities and paths taken by the members of a religious family are ignored.

A third strategy is inculturated pastoral activity. It is more something wished for than a work actually carried out. There is a lot of talk about it but not much is done. It is, however, the official position of the church. John Paul II urges it in his official teaching (particularly in *Catechesi Tradendae* and *Redemptoris Missio*) and on his many trips around the world. It also has the support of the Santo Domingo document (SD 252, 256, 279) and of church renewal in Bolivia, Mexico, Guatemala, and Brazil. There is reason for hope, but in order for it to be a reality, there must be careful planning and a reorientation of evangelization as a whole. The authoritarian and monocultural arrangements that have prevailed in our church (and in religious life) must be left behind. A growing sector of men and women religious are enthusiastic over this strategy of inculturated evangelization and what it means for the vowed life. Positive challenges are arising in personal community, apostolic, and spiritual terms.

In concluding this section, I ask which is preferable: Is it encouraging a religious life that is more "inserted" into each situation? Or is it being present and involved—as religious men and women—in the inculturating journey made by each church community? Such nuances are significant. The latter seems better and deeper to me, but it is well to move forward in the former as well. Insofar as we form part of an overall inculturating strategy by the church, each expression is enriched and transformed, including religious life.

CHARISMS IN CULTURAL PROCESSES

As we all know, living out the evangelical counsels is a "divine gift, which the Church has received from her Lord and which she ever preserves with the help of His grace" (LG 43). The standard is the gospel (PC 2); the life of the vows has well-defined characteristics (5); the renewal comes from the Spirit (2). This common heritage is realized in its own manner in Latin America.

Taking into account the teaching of the church and the worldwide and regional context, what is the charism of religious life? In our continent— and this is true in Asia, Africa, and elsewhere—renewed religious life has emphasized the option for the life of the poor and for a specific witness on behalf of the reign. As Victor Codina says: "A religious life . . . lives the Reign to its full extent, internally, eschatologically, ecclesially, and in collective history" and "Only out of the option of the poor can one today be a sign of the Reign, that is, be evangelizing."[5] To all of this must be added striving for inculturation. The charism of religious life is fidelity to the reign (present in and transcending our limited cultures) and to the Spirit (who guides each people along its human paths).

Making a connection between charism (of the religious life) and inculturation is relatively new, but it has been present implicitly. In the renewal of the religious life during recent decades we have returned to being centered on Christ and his reign. Thus sectarian positions and self-exaltation by religious, which have no biblical basis, are being overcome. It is also quite clear that founding charisms are being seen in a new light and the history of each particular order or congregation is receiving a Latin American rereading. A further thrust toward inculturation (although it is not called such) is reinvigorated spirituality, with methods and celebrations that are set within our own reality. We also have many communities living in the midst of the poor majority that are rediscovering evangelization with their feet on the ground and are providing religious life with a new foundation out of a life shared with the poor.

It is particular groups that are engaging in this experience, not the bulk of religious orders and congregations. Within our orders and congregations, little or nothing has been done to draw out indigenous, black, or mestizo identities. The gender perspective, the challenges of modernity, and the crisis of civilization are not being taken on. Much remains implicit; sometimes it is concealed and repressed, and sometimes it is shared timidly, out of fear of being misunderstood and being made outcast.

BIBLICAL PERSPECTIVE

Let us again take up the fundamental point: charismatic inspiration provided by religious life with its inculturated and intercultural dynamics. Because the charismatic is often distorted by fundamentalism, it is good idea to return to its sources in the Bible and see its implications in some emerging cultural processes.

The meaning of *grace* and *charisms* is set within the freely offered salvation that God grants to humankind; it is a grace accepted by the church community, which is at the service of every human being. Thus the charismatic is not something extraordinary, nor is it the property of unbalanced individuals. Quite the contrary, the people of God receives the charismatic in an ordinary and everyday manner and is its bearer. (Hence, the focus should not be solely on 1 Corinthians 12-14.) Another error is attributing the charismatic solely to some groups or some cultures. The charismatic has typified the entire church in its presence in Jewish and Gentile milieux, and thereafter in various places throughout the world in communities and hierarchies, in ministries, charisms, and institutions.

Grace is the source of Christian life and activity. It comes from the Spirit. Stephen's faith, wisdom, power, and courage, for example, come from the Spirit (Acts 6:3, 5, 10, 7:55), and he has grace (Acts 6:8). The same is true of Paul: he acts as a result of the gift received (Rom 12: 3, 1 Cor 3:10, Eph 5:7); likewise the churches, such as the one in Macedonia that is so generous (2 Cor 8:1). The fact that charism is gift and action enables us to visualize the charism of religious life not only as an individual and institutional treasure (in each congregation and order) but also as a driving force in our witness within each cultural process and in every human activity.

This perspective is ratified by texts that connect charism with strength, and texts that point to services prompted by the Spirit for the common good. Charism is a gift that strengthens (Rom 1:11, 1 Cor 1:7-8, Eph 3:7). It is, moreover, a strength that is not for oneself but for the church community and for human well-being (1 Cor 12:7, 1 Pt 4:10, 1 Tm 4:14, 2 Tm 1:6); for married life and for celibacy (1 Cor 7:7). The New Testament offers us several lists of charismatic services, works of the Spirit.[6]

Charisms are multiple, and they complement one another. The heart of what is charismatic is love; it is the main thing and includes all charisms (1 Cor 12:31—13:13). This is what moves us religious men and women to carry out our lives in the midst of the great human concert of love and of the gifts distributed by the Spirit in the church and throughout the people of God.

EMERGING PROCESSES

The power of charism present in human events and in the church community also challenges and inspires identities that are emerging in the present world context, as we can observe particularly in religious life.

At the outset, it is well to recall how much liberating and inculturated charism (although it may not have been called such) has already been part of the journeying of our peoples. That is demonstrated in Latin America by the existence of many kinds of Christianity that practice solidarity. A specific example here in the Andes is the gift of sharing and structured reciprocity.

In religious life there are many experiences of insertion into the worlds of the poor resulting from gospel charism. These experiences prize "being with" the poor and their cultures. This involves taking on their changing identities and their life projects. In putting into practice and reflecting on the following of Christ and fidelity to the reign, inculturation has taken place (even if not explicitly). The accents on gospel spirituality in living in the Spirit have also had the effect of transforming cultures.

National and international coordinating bodies (CONFER and CLAR) have served to draw together and encourage all of this.[7] Meanwhile, these questions are being deepened in liberation theology. N. Zevallos and V. Codina have proposed that "the Latin American people—impoverished whites, indigenous, blacks, poor mestizos, and mulattos—can enter religious life as an expression of a gospel option."[8] Although these sectors, particularly mestizos, are present in many congregations, their own features have been suppressed and concealed by the establishment of a uniform pattern that denies particular features (especially Afro-American and indigenous). The goal now is that those sectors, besides being brought into congregations, may also contribute their charisms, their own cultural and spiritual qualities. No one need hide or crush his or her roots. To the contrary, being able to be a religious with one's own particularity is enriching for all and grants each person self-esteem. This is about more than roots, but it is primarily about emerging cultural processes. As a result of the combination of the modern and the native-grown, and of interculturality, identities acquire new forms. Religious life can be inculturated in the midst of these processes.

It is an uphill battle. The overall context is unfavorable. The winds blowing in today's world arriving with the hurricane of progress and modernity are of cultural leveling. In church circles an imposed centralizing order is seeking to prevent inculturation from moving forward. Even so, steps are being taken in many places, as was evident in the 1994 World Synod of Bishops on religious life. In his exhortation, *Vita Consecrata*, John Paul II noted that the challenge of inculturation entails cooperating with God's grace in dealing with the diversity of cultures; he also said that vowed persons see the features of God's presence in the histories of peoples; and he warned that it is the role of the Holy See to accept or not to accept the results of inculturation.[9] This is a constant; inculturation is supported only cautiously. Even so, many are unwilling to accept inertia. Some international congregations, including the Jesuits and the Passionists,[10] are reorganizing their life and work in terms of inculturation. Religious communities are doing the same at a local level.

What can be done? To my mind, the first thing to be done is to appreciate the scope of the charismatic throughout the people of God. Religious life ought to join up with the deep charismatic currents existing in the laity and the hierarchy and provide its own proper and necessary impulses. It would be untrue to say that the charismatic is concentrated in religious life. Rather, the Holy Spirit "distributes special graces among the faithful of every rank . . . charismatic gifts, whether they be the most outstanding or the most simple and widely diffused" (LG 12). In our Latin American situation, and specifically in the Andes, it is quite clear that the inculturation of the charisms of the Spirit takes place in communities. There they bud, flower, and offer countless gifts of the Lord; of that we give witness and we collaborate with the process as religious men and women.

Some tasks and opportunities are proper to the vowed life. I mention them, keeping in mind the cultural processes surrounding us. Obviously each situation and the ongoing history of each institution will present tasks and opportunities for prayer and action. Here I only present some general elements.

The manifestations of the Spirit have their places and moments. These factors of space and time influence the development of charisms. It can be said that the vowed life is set within the experience of each community and people. In the setting of Andean modernity, here and now we must discern the signs of the reign and the signs in opposition to God's reign. We also share in moments of intensity, in both suffering and celebration; in qualitative terms these directions bring us into contact with the paschal process experienced by the people of the Andes. This is how religious life is inscribed in the portion of space and time where God is manifest to God's people.

All this entails particular details: food, housing, transportation, means of healing, clothing, family and neighborhood relations, economic organization, associations, and many other things. In such details one is making options, whether for dehumanizing patterns and their subtle idolatry or for the cultural creativity of each people that values life. In each detail of life one may accept alienation or wager on what is liberating. In our Andean world, for example, we religious can converse, cook, and celebrate with the authentic traits of a joyful people, or we can remain chained to patterns of success and competitiveness that split the community.

Apostolic activities may express inculturated charisms at the service of the people who are seeking life but who stumble into the pitfalls of the globalized system. Many poor people abandon their cultural energies and devote themselves to imitating alienating patterns. Here evangelization and the witness of a vowed life have a great responsibility. Do we enhance the positive community identities and self-esteem of people who suffer from fragmentation and marginalization? Do we remove from their class and culture people who receive our apostolic services and those who enter religious life? These questions are delicate and urgent in the way we deal with Andean youth, because they are the ones most vulnerable to homogenizing copycat "progress." Youth are led to imitate first-world patterns, and they are made alike so they will only aspire to having certain goods. Much remains to be done in this field so that the emerging aspirations of young people may build a new humankind. It seems to me that each of our works, services, and ministries can be evaluated on whether it has the spirit of mammon, or is inspired by the Spirit of love.

The challenges of inculturation also touch matters of internal organization, financing, planning, and formation programs. Sometimes prevailing criteria are pragmatic and thoughtless: that the order or congregation be successful and increase its power in contemporary society. This is very different from the gospel option and from encouraging the charism of each order or congregation: brotherly and sisterly spirit, effective and liberating apostolate, austerity and solidarity with the poor, becoming part of their yearnings for fullness of life, formation to follow Christ, a sound economic structure in each order or congregation, and collaboration within a shared and deeply spiritual "culture of life."

A FINAL WORD

I end by again expressing confidence that charisms in Latin American religious life are for the common good. They are not the private property of a congregation or of any church body. Rather, they are services that are signs of the salvation that God grants to humankind. As Camilo Maccise has said, the spirituality of religious life "has been enriched with the insistence on the diversity of charisms in the people of God."[11] The charisms themselves thus interact with and contribute to the charisms of others. Hence the vowed life ought not to be separated from church communities, nor should it be separated from the hierarchy. The gifts of the Spirit to one and all are for the common good. I also think that, inasmuch as it responds to the saving presence of the Lord in human history, inculturation is a gift of the Spirit. This gift has been transmitted to us, men and women religious, located in the midst of the charismatic and inculturating people of God.

In Pauline terms, the one thing that matters is the charism of love. The Spirit of love is encountered in communion with others and in the self-esteem that is life-building; it is not found in self-exaltation and in making an idol of progress, both of which disfigure modernity. This charism of love challenges the journey of our peoples. Latin American endeavors suffer the impact of neocolonial conditions (financial world, entertainment industry, patterns imposed on youth, and cynicism about politics). But some hope-giving lines are now emerging. Andean youth are devising their own ways of sharing, celebrating, and organizing their lives in interaction with other cultural processes. Modern progress is accepted, but it is not absolutized, because mestizo and native-grown wisdoms are being appreciated anew. They are also going beyond modernity, by transforming it and creating small-scale alternatives. This is obvious in art, new community processes, joy and solidarity, and many symbols that point toward a life in fullness.

Thanks to the charism of love, emerging cultural processes and inculturations of the faith will continue to offer marvelous fruits in Latin America and everywhere. One must say, "Thanks be to God!" The Spirit brings it about that the vowed life is one of many charisms of love as peoples make their pilgrimage. It is a sign, not for itself, but for the new human-kind, here and now among us in Latin America. Is the sign clear? That is what we hope and what has begun to flourish anew, thanks to the charism of love.

7

Catholic Identity
and the Good News Today

Our advances often occur through intuitions, certainties of the heart, spiritual sensitivities. That can be seen in the small journey of each individual person, and we can observe it in major Christian events. At Santo Domingo (1992) the Latin American and Caribbean bishops boldly and intuitively proposed inculturation. Like a baby born prematurely, its weakness requires special care; its future is insecure, but we trust and pray that it will continue to grow.

Certain concerns are arising around this issue. Why is it now that inculturation is being proposed to us? Is it a superficial fashion? Or is it redirecting the church's entire activity? Is it calling us to conversion, to a beautiful oasis of grace, to a *kairos*?

At the outset of his universal ministry John Paul II announced to us a "new time . . . a time of waiting" (RH 1). He then invited us to look to the long run, with ears open to the Spirit: "sensitivity to all that the Spirit says to the church and to the churches" (1994, *Tertio Millenio Adveniente* 23). Even so, backward-looking and uniformity-seeking Catholic fundamentalisms are spreading. They invoke discipline and doctrine to impede inculturation.

Some genuine concerns have to do with human responsibility on our planet, which has become globalized under modernity. As believers and as inculturated evangelizers, is our mission primarily moral and spiritual? In the face of so much skepticism about human ability to organize the world, and in the face of so much mediocrity, are we willing to risk ourselves for the sake of an inculturated and full liberation? Issues related to ecology and emotional life are also extremely urgent: How do we take charge of an earth that has been plundered? How do we heal a humankind that is confused and wounded? In short, as we take up the issue of inculturation, our concerns are quite broad.

Whose questions are most on target? In the face of secularism, some ask how we build Christian cultures. It is generally assumed that those in leadership positions are responsible for inculturation. They are concerned about their share of power. Likewise, those who consider themselves more educated and qualified try to fill what is missing and correct errors within modernity. Such concerns are those of elites more or less set apart from the rest of the Latin American population.

I prefer the questions raised by the many who are not heard. Their statements are accompanied by signs of dignity. For example, even though the poor are dependent on, and even subservient to, the powerful, they are suspicious of the existing institutional order (given its ineffectiveness and inhumanity) and question it. In a number of ways the people trace out alternative lines: Progress is fine, but who will it serve? Without faith what can we do? In whom can we trust? Moreover, popular Catholicism provides lessons in how to live an inculturated Christianity here and now. Thus we ask ourselves: How is the inculturated Good News received in the heart of our poor and believing peoples? In view of the current hyperculture of the worldwide market, what does the Good News passed on by communities of solidarity have to say? What is the proclamation of life in the midst of so many ways of being Latin American?

In our image-conscious civilization cosmetic makeovers are constantly being applied, and that obscures the situation in the church. Quickly and irresponsibly an attractive name is attached to anything. For example, a simple adaptation is called inculturation. Some evangelization programs are full of empty words. We very much need honesty—and occasionally we actually get it: "We have not known how to encourage the inculturation of the gospel in the Andean world, whether because of our fear, our inability to understand, or our idealization of cultures."[1]

Little by little, since the 1977 synod, inculturation has been entering into the papal magisterium: *Catechesi Tradendae* (1979); more so in *Redemptor Hominis* 1; in numerous pastoral programs, bishops statements, works of theology, renewals in religious life; and in lay activities and movements.

Inculturation was a thread winding through the Fourth General Conference of Bishops in Santo Domingo (Message of Santo Domingo 18-22, 32, 38; SD 13, 15, 24, 30, 33, 43, 49, 53, 55, 58, 84, 87, 102, 128, 177, 224, 228-262, 292-303). To what extent is this great proposal being implemented and deepened? Is it just a label? Is it a pastoral strategy?

To the extent that we take up inculturation, we are reaffirming our Catholicism, which is multicultural. It has been said that Vatican II marked out a new period: the presence of the church on a world scale. Our Latin American church ought not be so tied to patterns of Christianity in the developed world. Fidelity to the Spirit leads us over the paths of inculturation. To follow, we have to take today's realities into account.

GLOBALIZATION AND CATHOLICITY

Inculturation is not shut up within the customs of each little corner of humankind. Each situation is affected by the globalization of life. In gospel terms, the Lord is pressing us to "proclaim the Good News to all creation" (Mk 16:15). So how does the task of inculturation influence the march of history in the world? How does being Catholic demand an inculturation?

WORLD DYNAMICS

Each people's identity and the features of its historic journey are set within a worldwide civilization, modernity which has become globalized.

Let us first note some local aspirations and then observe some global processes. My starting point is the situation in the Andes, because that is where I am.

Almost all people and groups in the Andes have set themselves the goal of "getting ahead" by studying, pursuing a profession, migrating for better work and living conditions, technologies, media, and comprehending the world. People tend to favor the English language and like to use computers. What is going on? Have people in the Andes gotten on board the rocket of modernity and abandoned their own imaginative construction of this earth? Are they losing their culture, becoming cultureless? If we observe the facts, we find that there are many processes of mestizaje, biculturality, and inter- action among various symbolic universes.

In general, the peoples of Latin American enter into the realms of moder- nity with their own goals and values, and they are transforming it. Throughout the continent we have the "hemidernal" (semi-modern), as Cristián Parker calls it.[2] That is, our peoples both are and are not modern. They assume modernity, and yet they also question it and surpass it. In some areas they are creative and free; in other areas the general pattern is to mimic alienating and dehumanizing patterns. All this presents challenges to inculturation, which is carried out by human beings who are both particu- lar and worldwide, with their own logics and cultural pluralism.

Global processes do not affect the world system in a uniform way, al- though everything is interconnected. Actually, particular cultures are being reaffirmed in the midst of the conditions of modernity. These processes are quite complex, and they can be viewed in various ways.[3] We are facing a new age, which Xavier Gorostiaga says is "more a change of era than an era of changes." Renato Ortiz explains that along with homogenization there are phenomena of segmentation and diversification, and that with moder- nity the diversity of popular cultures is actually enhanced. For their part, representatives of the world's religions emphasize the ethical aspect vis-à- vis the global crisis and call for a new global order that requires a global ethic.

Some features of our age are alarming, while others are positive. Vast areas are excluded and kept in subjection: almost all of Africa, parts of Asia, a great deal of the Caribbean and Latin America. Plans for economic and political development are being elaborated (now that issues of security in a bipolar world have been left behind), but when we evaluate decades of development we see that few sectors have moved ahead and most people remain stuck. Yet there are worldwide dynamics of communications, computers, specialized education, the acceleration of science and technology, environmental concerns, and a very clear entry of women onto the scene. In short, we stand before a change of era.

These processes can be worked and understood from below, out of the cultures and masses enduring discrimination, among whom there is a great human quality and power of belief. These processes are challenged by the Good News, which overcomes the powers of death. In this regard there should be a discernment of everything that is happening today, a discernment carried out with the eyes and heart of Jesus Christ and his church. In other words, inculturation deals with worldwide processes, and this is part of the option of the poor on behalf of life.

All this entails rethinking what it means to be Catholic and to act Catholic. We live our faith within peoples involved in their own specific reality and in worldwide processes.

BEING CATHOLIC TODAY

In Latin America the Catholicism of ordinary people displays a great deal of inculturation, while official church bodies—paradoxically and regrettably—are less inculturated.

To begin with, being Catholic is very much rooted in the everyday struggle to live. Striking examples are social and religious celebrations, with patterns of human interchange, stratification and leadership, celebratory forms, religious rites, and devotions to images.[4] In saying "I'm a Catholic," many people implicitly mean that they take part in feast days of the people. Such things are signs of being Catholic, just as much as the fact of being baptized and going to some church. A very common distinction is whether one believes in the saints and the Virgin or not. But behind such opinions are underlying issues: Catholic inculturations with their successes, limits, and ambivalences. Another major sign is the institution of the social and spiritual association: groups devoted to a saint, catechetical circles, lay movements, pilgrimages to shrines, biblical prayer and charismatic groups, Christian base communities. In addition, people have established connections with centers of power: Catholic sponsored education and media, or agencies run by ecclesiastics and religious congregations. There is yet one more thing that I regard as crucial: the correlation among different human traditions. This is the reason that Catholics continue to cultivate a religiosity that is culturally mestizo, indigenous, black, of the Amazon, or with some Asian elements (and often a certain combination of these things). We thus have particular types of inculturation of the faith. Indeed, there is a great potential for evangelization in the ways in which the people are Catholic. Furthermore, modern civilization favors cultural pluralism, and that offers spaces for different features of Catholicism.

Second, pastoral work along the lines of the conciliar renewal seems to have many limitations. One can find this in every part of the continent. Conservative ways of engaging in pastoral work can also be evaluated (for example, reproducing patterns from other periods and other times); the lack of authenticity is plain to see. But we are more concerned with the broad current of renewal resulting from Vatican II and the ecclesial vitality from Medellín to the present.

In this broad current we find all kinds of things. I limit myself to two issues. Faced with the challenges of globalization, on the one hand, and particular identities, on the other, we do not have a strategy for evangelization and inculturation. That is why many people seek and find other routes (the new religious movements, a Christianity without participation in the church, and so forth). It is true that there is a great deal of generosity and spirituality in the renewal current. But little has been achieved by way of evangelizing cultures. Certainly evangelizing efforts among the middle classes display accomplishments and plans. It is the sensibilities, thoughts, and projects of the middle classes that are most present in social pastoral work, direct aid, human development, sacramental catechesis, movements of spirituality, Latin American theology, and lay associations. Hence it can be said that pastoral work has a monocultural tendency coming from the middle sectors and that the development of catholicity is thereby hindered. Other cultural and religious ways are consequently growing because they have other roots and inculturated horizons, and because they are in tune with the needs and sensitivities of the popular strata.

Another major Catholic issue has to do with emerging subjects and Latin American identities. If we stand at a change of era, very clear challenges have to be faced. New subjects have emerged: young people, with their cultural energies; women with their relational and holistic way of being; Afro-American populations; indigenous communities; poor urban associations; socially responsible sectors of business; neo-political leaders. Some of these subjects are present (often passively) in the programs of the Catholic church, but they are comparatively small in number (when compared with such sectors as a whole). Only exceptionally are these subjects with their identities shaping renewed pastoral work.

One aspect of this issue is the mismatch between forms of spirituality and religious worlds. Being Catholic involves greater interreligious communication and collaboration. There is a need to recognize God in the different religious paths and in humanist currents. What is required, as the Jesuits say, is "contemplation of God working in everything, which helps us to discern the divine spirit in religions and cultures."[5] With regard to the Andean region, it is obvious that there is a mismatch between the official level and the life of faith of the people. Despite five hundred years of church presence in the world of the Andes, we still do not have—on the official level—an inculturation in church structure, ethics, the sacraments and liturgy, and ministry. The people do, however, have their own ways of inculturating faith in the Andean human process.

To conclude this point, the task is to evangelize globalized human existence, taking into account its lights and shadows. We are evangelized and we evangelize reciprocally as modern citizens, with our characteristic features and our pluralism. In other words, inculturation is both local and global. Being Catholic must not be understood as being sectarian (in competition with other religions). Thank God, popular Catholicism has achieved many inculturations and today it is relevant in settings of modernity. Yet post-renewal pastoral work, despite some small successes, comes up short in many areas; it is not in tune with nor does it respond to the huge challenges of the era in which we find ourselves. Despite the values and potential that exist, there are deep-seated problems that cannot be concealed.

MISSTEPS AND SUCCESSES IN INCULTURATION

A low-level debate is taking place in our church circles. Many assume that inculturation is about places where there are indigenous and black people, and little thought is given to the range of mestizo situations, which quantitatively and culturally are the most significant in our continent (the Santo Domingo text mentions mestizaje only superficially). Another blind spot is the failure to see the challenges to inculturation from modernity in both the city and the countryside. On this matter the document of the bishops in Santo Domingo does indeed offer observations that are on target. A further refinement should be made, however, in the sense that the message cannot be inculturated into modern culture (in the singular). Rather, the point is to communicate the Good News in the various arrangements of manifold modern civilization. Evangelization is done not in a single setting but in a variety of modern contexts. A simplistic way of connecting gospel and culture without including its religious aspects is another topic that merits discussion. In the Andean world, for example, communicating the gospel entails entering into dialogue with native as well as syncretist religions that include already inculturated elements of Christian faith. In short, some matters deserve discernment and discussion; quick and irresponsible procedures are out of place.

Here I discuss what I call hyper-inculturation and poly-inculturation. These concerns spring out of specific work; that is where they are verified and worked out with the contribution of the entire people of God.

A HYPER-INCULTURATION

In the midst of the wonderful advances of modernity we find ourselves facing a totalitarian presence of the market, which makes its way (sometimes subtly, sometimes aggressively) into the imaginative construction of the world and behavior of each people. Almost everything is completely changed: the human body is reified, time becomes banal ("time is money"), while illness, love, spirituality, and many other things are incorporated into the framework of monetary costs and returns. In making this observation, one also has to recognize what is positive about the market, which is part of the advance of humankind. Nevertheless, it often becomes an absolute and a one-dimensional value. Persons and things are victims of such reductionism. This is not primarily a moral problem, but rather the problem is that we are surrounded by an overarching planetary culture that is present in every corner of life.

The religious terrain is also affected by frameworks of supply and demand, capitalization and appropriation of spiritual goods, competition among religious bodies, and reinterpretation of the sacred as guarantee of material success and individual dignity. This paradigm is also used in our Christian churches. We naively use methods, strategies, and concepts defined by the overarching market culture. One even hears talk of advertising and selling the image of Jesus Christ.

This I call a hyper-inculturation. It has a vast capability of encompassing everything, and it does so deeply. That is why I call it "hyper." Can it be considered an inculturation? I believe so, because (whether we like it or not) it is a way of living, understanding, and communicating the gospel carried out by church people and organizations. They work out their communication of the Christian gospel convinced of their own faith and with a sense of solidarity with others. A radical critique can be made of their actions, but there is no point in disqualifying the faith of spokespersons and their adherents; nor would it be just to demonize them with the claim that they are agents of mammon. For myself, I join those who question this paradigm on the basis of the pain and hope of the poor and according to criteria that are theologically based. To my mind, this is a biased and wrong kind of inculturation.

As an example, I take what is proposed by Antonio Kater Filho, an executive at a television company of the Charismatic Renewal in Brazil.[6] It is a model of evangelization set clearly in the logic and vicissitudes of the market. Kater assures those who have reservations that it is not a profanation and that capitalist culture is not incompatible with the gospel.

Here is the basic framework. Marketing consists of four factors: product, price, plaza (market), and promoting sales. Kater states categorically that Catholic participation in church is dropping off while sects and other Christian and non-Christian religions are growing. But there is a deeper reason for marketing: Christ and eternal salvation are the best product in the world. On that basis Kater reviews sacred history, showing how Jesus, Paul, and saints over the course of history have been successful at marketing(!). He cites Paul VI, canon law, and the new Catholic catechism. Evangelization is regarded as a model for companies today. The church must accordingly use techniques and strategies from business marketing. Such marketing detects the unmet needs of humankind. He then quickly and efficiently presents the product, eternal salvation, along with a "promotion" strategy. He does so through "outlets," which are parishes, and especially through television, which reaches multitudes.

In this paradigm the people are regarded as a "marketing target" in a religious sense, and the target is that they have faith in eternal salvation. This goal has to be attained. Thus, no attention is paid to the message of new life in Christ, nor is there a call to discipleship in a church that is the sacrament of the salvation of humankind. Nor is there a dialogue with different cultures and with the spiritualities of today. It seems to me that evangelization suffers grave distortions in this overarching cultural framework. The market is not subjected to a gospel discernment. The people are not regarded as bearers of the faith. Their problems and their vital needs are manipulated. In short, the Good News is disfigured and misdirected by being run through marketing channels. In the words of a spokesperson for this movement: "We always had two great products, Jesus and salvation; what was lacking was selling them directly."[7]

This model may strike us as an extreme and isolated case, but actually many people apply it with moderate formulas that go unnoticed. In our church there are many methods for spreading the message in which we do not interact with the cultures and spiritual sensitivities of the Latin American people. Unfortunately, very often it happens that the presence of God is not seen in the journey of each people, and an attempt is made to evangelize on the basis of human powers. Thus what happens is a hyper-inculturation, or better, a cultural imposition that claims to bear the gospel. That is not in keeping with the heart of the gospel—saving dialogue between God and God's people so that they may live in fullness.

A MULTIPLE INCULTURATION

In the renewal of the church in Latin America we have been refining our approaches. In the 1970s and 1980s we talked about well-educated cultures and popular cultures (without the necessary nuances, and without setting them within processes of globalization). Subsequently, in the 1980s and 1990s, we uncovered mosaics, the complexity of intercultural contacts, processes of change, Latin American heterogeneity, and symbolic realities. Hence inculturation is not pictured as a simple relationship between two entities; for example, conceiving of the one communicating a message as one pole and the cultural recipient as the other. Moreover, here in the Americas we are observing how people move about within two or more cultural processes and are bicultural or intercultural. The Good News is received with the mediations of modernity that are proper to a country with transnational elements and with mestizo identities or other ways of being. It is on these complex terrains that inculturation and interculturation take place. We are

also becoming aware that human development is inseparable from a multitude of cultural and spiritual forms. Straight-line, androcentric, and monocultural development is increasingly being subject to criticism.

The church community is beginning to hear voices of subjects who have
their own symbols, ideas, and overarching designs. We are hearing what is
being said by cultures emerging in the cities. These are voices from migrants, with their new associations and their own particular dramas; from
the cultures of young people, who are the majority; from the relational
identity and proposal for a humane life made by women; from the worri-
some situation of the environment.

In short, the different identities and cultural processes force us to raise
the issue of multiple inculturation. This is in agreement with the multicultural
nature of Catholicism as it is lived in Latin America and the Caribbean.
Moreover, since its origins the Good News was proclaimed to Jews and
Gentiles, to weak and strong, to women and men, and was not imprisoned
by one cultural framework. It has been in dialogue with all.

We also have encouraging guidelines issued by the bishops who met in
Santo Domingo (even though the reception of this magisterium is slow and
timid). Puebla considered the evangelization of cultures; to it is now added
the proposal for inculturation. Santo Domingo devotes more attention to
modern and urban culture, education, and the media (SD 252-262, 277-
286). The most novel element is the treatment of the indigenous and
Afro-American dimension (243-251); the mestizo dimension is mentioned
only in passing. Throughout the document one of the three major pastoral
themes is inculturated evangelization (292, 297-303). The expression "Christian culture" is used, but it is not in the foreground (see 13, 22, 24, 31, 33,
45, 97, 229, 263). This formula is aimed at sacralizing a particular way of
living within modernity; it is, however, a proposal that cannot work in our
pluralistic world. On the whole, the Santo Domingo event served to publi-
cize inculturation; unfortunately, little interest in the issue has been evident
after Santo Domingo. The baby was born, but it is now stumbling about.

It is well to see how Santo Domingo connects this issue to the calling to
freedom. There are two very clear texts: Inculturation is an "effort [that]
takes place . . . within the striving and aspiration of each people, strengthening its identity and liberating it from the powers of death" (SD 13), and
"One goal of inculturated evangelization will always be . . . salvation and
integral liberation" (243). Thus the traditional preference for the poor is
being deepened. As a result of the Santo Domingo event, that option of the
Latin American church is combined within initiatives of peoples of these
lands ("striving and aspiration of each people"), with identities and projects
of city people, mestizos, indigenous people, Afro-Americans, and all this
takes into account the great thrust of modernity.

By way of example, I mention the southern Andean region of Peru. The
inculturating energies in the hands of the communities and grassroots leaders

are striking. Many have appreciated the everyday existence of Quechua, Aymara, and mestizo Christianities with their corresponding religious symbols. Today we are also appreciative of the diversification of pastoral activities: peasants, women, health, young people solidarity and human rights, city pastoral work. All this entails a multiple inculturation.

A rich experience and understanding of God is also being worked out, as was evident in a theology workshop:

- "We think of God at the beginning of each day, at the start of work and when we travel."
- "We know how to ask and also how to be thankful because God always blesses us."
- "We think about God and we offer him our first fruits, we dance and eat together with everyone."
- "We ask forgiveness from God and from our brothers and sisters; that is what we grant so that God will listen to us."
- "These are difficult times. . . . There is more sin than before, but God is our defender and savior."
- "We can see both the light and the darkness."[8]

Here, as elsewhere, we observe concrete advances being made due to initiatives by a deeply Christian people. As Victor Codina keenly observes: "The poor people live their faith out of their culture, without either/ors and without overconcern for purity. Among the people inculturation is first a praxis before being any possible theory."[9] This clear-sightedness and creativity by "those on the bottom" is lacking in the church that claims to be renewed.

Thus far I have sketched out two major currents:

1. Evangelization with a one-sided cultural and economic mediation (the total market), which leads to hyper-inculturation.

2. Multidimensional inculturated evangelization carried out by Christian communities guided by the magisterium. The goal is an inculturated liberation. I have also stressed the inculturated faith lived and generated by peoples with their deep wisdom and spirituality.

As I have already said, the "reception" of Santo Domingo is slow and uneven. Its three major thrusts must be emphasized. Unfortunately, the tendency is to ignore and misinterpret the thrust of inculturation. Some people have a poor memory. As an example, I take the Pastoral Plan of Peru (1995-2000), drawn up "in the light of Santo Domingo, looking toward the third millennium."[10] This plan speaks primarily about a culture (shared, mestizo synthesis, Christian, Catholic, cf. 1, 2, 16, 51, 57, 62, 67, 84, 88), and only in passing does it mention inculturation (56, 67, 85). It is my impression that the newborn should be called by its proper name: *inculturation*. It has to be allowed to walk and to grow.

CONCLUSIONS

The inculturated Good News is communicated locally and universally. The catholicity of faith implies sacramental and saving presence in all cultures. A proposal for inculturation had been drawn together and elaborated at the Santo Domingo conference, but it is fragile. In practice, many do not take on this new dimension of the gospel option for poor peoples who are bearers of the gospel.

We need an inculturated ecclesio*logy* and ecclesio-*practice*. That began to be made explicit on the official and continent-wide level in 1992. Some texts that were suppressed at Santo Domingo[11] have to remain in our ecclesial memory:

Once these peoples have been constituted as agents of their own history of salvation, they will bring it about that the gospel, which has germinated in their cultures, will bloom as genuinely indigenous, Afro-American, and mestizo churches, which in full communion with the universal church will be able to transmit the saving message of Jesus Christ.

The church which evangelizes out of these cultures in an inculturated manner can prophetically show in them and offer to the world a great light and power of life and hope: a providential sign of the Kingdom of God who raises up and saves the entire universe out of those who are crucified in history.

In other words, along with the work of inculturation, it is the church itself that is called to be changed and to be founded anew. That is why the talk is of a genuinely mestizo, black, and indigenous ecclesiality. I insist that it is not enough that some actions of inculturation take place among native peoples. The underlying issue is that the local church is to live in an inculturated way and thereby be in communion with the universal church.

This is no doubt the result of major efforts and takes place over the long run, but the crucial element is the small steps that we take today and tomorrow. It is in these efforts that our fidelity (or infidelity) to the Spirit of Jesus crucified and risen is tested. From Pentecost to this day, it is the Spirit who sustains inculturation. It is up to the ecclesial community to respond to and collaborate with the Spirit of God. That means, as we all know, making efforts that go beyond mediocrity. Most of all, it involves being sensitive so as to listen and put into practice the "message of the Spirit to the churches" (Rv 2:7).

Conclusion

Today each cultural process interacts with globalized powers. That marks the everyday—where culture is created and reproduced—and also reshapes the proposal of inculturation. Some forces are seeking to impose uniformity, and they devalue and even destroy the particular and everyday. But there are also new reaffirmations. We can observe a technological, economic, and symbolic globalization; its counterpart is the reaffirmation of identities, of the being and action of each people. That is why, as the Christian event is being inculturated today, we deal with both globalized modernity and the various types of shared human life.

Throughout these pages I have sketched a historic process within which there is dawning a sense of an inculturated church. This key of inculturation opens many doors to our situation. We of course have other keys: sociopolitical; ecological; gender and generational; emotional and sexual; racial—indigenous, black, and mestizo; economic; and ethical. These are various ways of understanding and building an everyday reality. Each of these keys can be complementary to the others, and they make us more alert to a complex universe.

I have clarified misunderstandings. Inculturation is not the property of specialists; rather, it has to do with everything done, believed, and celebrated by God's people. Throughout these pages we have paused to consider a number of areas: evangelization efforts in the contexts of modernity, religion of the people, catechesis, education, mission, and religious life. It is the entire human journey (not just a few "cultural customs") and evangelization and thinking in faith that are the issues reopened by the key of inculturation. Good specialists do not isolate culture from everything else, much less reduce it to folklore. Good theology and pastoral work do not relegate cultural matters to "preliminaries" and to "concrete applications." They permeate all understanding and the proclamation and witness of the Christian faith. Theological and pastoral monologues are superficial. Deep dialogue must take place with each human identity and with overall cultural processes.

Upon reaching the end of these pages, each person can answer this question: How are peoples and churches in our continent experiencing the dawn as they engage in inculturation? Monocultural patterns are dehumanizing. In faith terms, we enjoy and give thanks for the love of God and human communion out of a beautiful mosaic of identities and life projects.

117

Inculturation is a radical gospel challenge. Are we faithful disciples of the Jesus Christ who was placed in the Jewish world and open to Samaritans and Gentiles? Are we moved by the freedom of St. Paul, a Christian without borders who was inculturated in each situation? Are we continuing to shape a genuinely catholic church, one that is multicultural, present in every human process, a sacrament of salvation in today's world out of the poor for whom God has opted? These are challenges that entail living the paschal event today.

Because it is the Spirit who guides inculturation, reading the "signs of the times" has a pneumatological cast. The signs of a change of epoch and of civilization seem to be opportunities opened by the Spirit to rebuild cultures of life. The Spirit also seems to be renewing the church in the mosaic of Latin American peoples who are journeying toward the kingdom of full joy. But we find ourselves in ambivalent situations; there are reversals and huge obstacles. Fundamentalist postures are seeking security and fleeing from the risk of inculturation. Often the aim of evangelizing culture is not backed up by institutional works and the everyday practice of the faith. We adjust to the spirit of this world, which is governed by one kind of material success.

Despite everything, the dawn continues advancing. It is something that takes in both the obscure and the luminous. Our sacramentally divine human journey has its colors. They are beautiful, dark, shaded, bright, brilliant, mysterious. They are also the colors of the inculturation that is being carried out thanks to the Spirit, who unceasingly inspires the Christian community. In the midst of shadows and bright light, the church experiences an ever-brighter dawn.

This happens even though we Latin American peoples are half asleep and feel the allure of today's idols. Yet dissatisfaction is growing, and some social and cultural alternatives are taking hold in some sectors of our continent. Many human communities treasure their identities and designs; the cultural uniformity brought by globalization is being challenged.

Finally, we are told that the goal of inculturation "will always be salvation and integral liberation" (SD 243). The statement is both prophetic and realistic. Yet, some retain the dream of a mighty Christian culture. That is not viable in the contemporary pluralistic context—except as a kind of refuge. Nor does it take on the tension between human history and the kingdom of God. Another unrealizable proposal is separating what is cultural from everything else and being devoted to evangelizing primarily culture and its religious core. It seems to me that the people of God realistically live their faith in the everyday and in the transcendent. They walk in a problematic land and yearn for peace in heaven. They know and celebrate salvation in the midst of darkness and light. Spirit-driven, inculturated forms of faith are a journey in the truth that makes us free.

Notes

1. PRACTICE AND THEOLOGY

1. See H. C. F. Mansilla, *Los Tortuosos Caminos de la Modernidad* (La Paz: CEBERM, 1992), p. 27; N. García C., *Políticas Culturales en América Latina* (Mexico: Grijalbo, 1987) (together with the metropolitan model of modernization, he notes the weight of the cultural in an alternative development, p. 23); Jorge Larraín, *Modernidad, Razón e Identidad en América Latina* (Santiago: Andrés Bello, 1996), a rigorous look at the debate on the modern.

2. This strategy is present in the 1977 consultation document for Puebla (309, 219-220, 638, 640, 643, 1027) and in 1989 in the consultation document for Santo Domingo (728, 731, 739, 755, 763, 1128), but in both instances "Christian culture" ended up being marginal in the final texts.

3. For Brazil, see *Cadernos do ISER* 21, 22, 23 (1989-90); for Peru, see the studies organized by the bishops, "Grupos religiosos contemporáneos no católicos en el Perú," first and second stage 1985-87 (Lima) (by U. Rodríguez, H. Muñoz, A. Sueiro, C. Romero).

4. A. Torres Q. *El Diálogo de las Religiones* (Santander: Sal Terrae, 1992), pp. 34-38.

5. Marilena Chauí, *Cultura e Democracia* (Sao Paulo: Cortez, 1989), p. 83.

6. Cristián Parker, "Fe popular y campo cultural," in *Por los Caminos de América* (Santiago: Paulinas, 1992), pp. 149, 183.

7. In Mexico the well-known twelve Franciscans associate God with the Spaniards and name God as "in teotl in tlatoami" (God with absolute political power). They engage in a colonial type of inculturation. As B. de Sahagún noted, the natives called Mary Tonantzin (Our Mother). The Nahuatl community carries out its own inculturation. See C. Duverger, *La Conversión de los Indios de la Nueva España* (Quito: Abya Yala, 1990), pp. 103, 118, 233; and X. Serrano, *Los Primeros 50 Años de Evangelización en el Mundo Nahuatl* (Mexico: La Cruz, 1991), pp. 22, 74.

8. "Inculturation" appears four times in the "Primera Redacción" (1989) and five times in the "Instrumento Preparatorio" (1990). After the "Prima Relatio" (1990), which pulls together the contributions from bishops' conferences, the "Doc. de Consulta" (1991) has "inculturation" in forty-eight paragraphs, and the "Secunda Relatio" (1982) has "inculturation" in sixty-seven paragraphs and "Christian culture" in eleven paragraphs. The "Doc. de Trabajo" (1992) has "inculturation" in twenty-eight paragraphs while "Christian culture" appears in nine paragraphs. The Santo Domingo document mentions "inculturation" in forty-one paragraphs and "Christian culture" in nine paragraphs. These statistics are significant. (In the text the three last documents are cited with the initials SR, DT, and SD.)

119

9. Paulo Suess, "Evangelización desde las culturas," in *Vida, Clamor y Esperanza* (Bogotá: Paulinas, 1992), pp. 221-238, and *Evangelizar a partir de los projectos históricos dos outros* (Sao Paulo: Paulus, 1995), pp. 121-144, 167-194, 213-237; F. Damen, *Hacia una Teología de la Inculturación* (La Paz: CRB, 1989), pp. 38-40; L. Boff, *Nova Evangelização* (Petrópolis: Vozes, 1990), pp. 62ff., 82-96; E. Cavassa, "Vivir de los de Dios de otro modo: inculturación y fe," *Páginas* 106 (1990), 22, 29, 31-38; N. Zeballos, "Cultura e Inculturación," in *La Nueva Evangelización* (Lima: CEP/IBC, 1992), pp. 75, 95-97; for inculturation and popular cultures see articles by Pedro Trigo and Ronaldo Muñoz, *Por los Caminos de América* (Santiago: Paulinas, 1992), pp. 273-302; and see review *Inculturación*, which began to be published by the Institute of Aymara Studies in Puno, Peru, in 1995.

10. Sketches of neo-Christendom can be found in A. Methol F., "El resurgimiento católico latinoamericano," *Religión y Cultura* (Bogotá: CELAM, 1981), pp. 63-124, and the report on the discussion at that event in J. Terán in the same volume, pp. 328-367; G. Carriquiry, "Cinco siglos de la Iglesia en A.L.," *Vida y Espiritualidad* (Lima) 22 (1992), pp. 35-62; P. Bigó, "La Iglesia L.A. frente a la mutación cultural de la modernidad" (Santiago: ILADES, 1988), pp. 11-22; P. Morandé in the same volume, "Modernidad y Cultura L.A.: desafíos para la Iglesia," and his "Comentario al tema propuesto para la IV Conferencia," *Vida y Espiritualidad* (Lima) 19 (1991), pp. 121-124. For the "reconciliation" school, see Germán Doig, *De Rio a Santo Domingo* (Lima: VE, 1993), pp. 84-90, 222-239; and presentations at the Fifth International Conference on Reconciliation, in the collection *Nueva Evangelización Rumbo al Tercer Milenio* (Lima: VE, 1996).

11. F. Sebastián A. *Nueva Evangelización* (Madrid: Encuentros, 1991), pp. 31, 81.

12. See. G. Remolina, "Problemática de la evangelización de la cultura hoy," and J. C. Scannone, "Pastoral de la cultura hoy en A.L." both in *Evangelización de la Cultura e Inculturación del Evangelio* (Buenos Aires: Guadalupe, 1988), pp. 99-100 and 270-274 respectively; Dom A. Do Carmo Cheuiche, *Evangelización de la Cultura e Inculturación del Evangelio* (Bogotá: CELAM, 1988), pp. 49-50; J. Comblin, "Perspectivas teológicas sobre la cultura," in *Teología y Cultura* (Santiago: Sociedad Chilena de Teologia, 1992), pp. 6-15; J. Silva, "Evangelización y Cultura," in *Por los Caminos de América,* pp. 332-342.

13. Parables of the everyday as sign of the kingdom: Mk 4:26-29, Mt 13:24-33, 44-50, 18:23-35, 20:1-6, 22:1-14, 25:1-13. Biting and paradoxical proverbs: Lk 9:60, 62, Mk 3:24-26, Mt 5:44, 7:13-14, etc.

14. See Lk 9:1-9, 10:2-11, Mt 28:18-20, Lk 24:47, Jn 16:13, 20:22, Acts 1:8.

15. I. Gebara, "Presencia de lo feminino," in *Cambio Social y Pensamiento Cristiano en América Latina* (Madrid: Trotta, 1993), pp. 210-211. G. Montilius, "Dios y lo sagrado," in *Cultura Negra y Teología* (San José: DEI, 1986), p. 163. El López, "Caminar Teológico de los Pueblos Indios," presentation in Guatemala (1992), p. 10. P. Trigo, "El futuro de la teología de liberación," in *Cambio Social,* pp. 309-313. V. Serrano, *Teología de la Ecología* (Quito: Abya Yala, 1991), p. 23.

16. G. Gutiérrez, "Sobre el Documento de Consulta para Puebla," *Páginas* 16-17 (1978), pp. 6-7, 18-20. S. Silva, "Teología y Cultura," in *Por los Caminos . . .* p. 196. L. Boff, *Nova Evangelização,* pp. 24, 122-126. J. C. Scannone, ibid., p. 271.

17. See Trigo, "El futuro," and Gebara, "Presencia de lo feminino."

18. Cf. F. L. C. Teixeira, *Comunidades Eclesiales de Base, Bases Teológicas* (Petrópolis: Vozes, 1988), pp. 119-121. CLAR, *La Vida Según el Espíritu:*

Comunidades Religiosas de América Latina (Bogotá: CLAR, 1977). José Comblin, *The Holy Spirit and Liberation* (Maryknoll, N.Y.: Orbis Books, 1989). Victor Codina, *Creo en el Espíritu Santo* (Santander: Sal Terrae, 1994).

19. The great paradigm of evangelizing cultures (Vatican II, *Evangelii Nuntiandi,* Puebla) is taken further with proposals for inculturation: *Catechesi Tradendae* (1979), 46, 53; *Slavorum Apostoli* (1995), 21-26; *Redemptoris Missio* (1991), 52; extraordinary synod (1985), part II, D, 4, "Christian Freedom and Liberation," of the Congregation of the Doctrine of the Faith (1986), 96; SD 228-230, 143-285.

20. See *Voices from the Third World* (June 1979); Pro Mundi Vita, *La Política de Inculturación en Asia Oriental* 104 (1986/11); Aloysius Pieris, "A Theology of Liberation in Asian Churches," in *Liberation in Asia* (Delhi: Vidyajyoti, 1987), pp. 17-38; J. M. Waliggo, et al., *Inculturation* (Kampala: Uganda, 1986); A. Shorter, *Toward a Theology of Inculturation* (New York: Paulist, 1990); P. Schineller, *Handbook on Inculturation* (New York: Paulist, 1990); N. Bitoto Abeng, "Are Attempts at the Inculturation of Christianity in Africa Failing?" *Concilium* 5 (1990); M. M'nteba, "La inculturatcion en the third church" *Concilium* 239 (1992), 169-189; R. Schreiter, "A Framework for a Discussion of Inculturation," in *Mission in Dialogue* (Maryknoll, N.Y.: Orbis Books, 1982), pp. 544-556.

21. D. Ribeiro claims that in our history outside influences called for making things uniform in the economic and political realms: "Latin American Culture," *Cuadernos de Cultura Latinoamerica* (Mexico, 1970); some outside forces linked to internal factors also operate in this way in matters of religion.

22. Congregation for the Evangelization of Peoples, "Dialogue and Proclamation" (Rome 1991), no. 29-30 (and *Redemptoris Missio,* 28-29).

23. *Obras del P. José de Acosta*, "De procuranda indorum salute," BAE, vol. 73 (Madrid, 1954), book I (pp. 407-408) and book V.

2. SOURCES: INCARNATION, PASCH, AND PENTECOST

1. The statistics are significant: in 1900 34.4% of all human beings were Christian; in 1992 the figure was 33.4% (a total of 1,833,022,000 people, of whom 998,900,000 were Catholic, figures from the *International Bulletin of Missionary Research,* 16/1). In other words, throughout this century the percentage of Christians has remained almost the same. In 1992, the total of other believers could be broken down as follows: Muslim, 988,004,000; nonreligious, 897,520,000; Hindu, 736,127,000; Buddhist, 330,498,000; atheist, 238,968,000; new religions, 121,724,000; tribal religions, 99,646,000; Sikhs, 19,289,000; Jews 18,011,000.

2. Cardinal José Sanchez says that the catechism is a "thorough attempt to inculturate the faith . . . in the realm of the universal church" (*L'Osservatore Romano* 1226 [April 4, 1993]).

3. For example, Germán Doig, *De Rio a Santo Domingo* (Lima: VE, 1993) speaks a great deal about Christian culture (231, 141, 201, 242), and on only one occasion (while quoting the pope) he speaks of inculturation (132).

4. See Paul Poupard, *Las Religiones* (Barcelona: Herder, 1989), especially p. 131.

5. For an overview of syncretism, see C. Parker, *Otra Lógica en América Latina* (Mexico-Chile: FCE, 1993), pp. 27-36, 366-369, 375-382; for case studies, see A. R. Martynow and G. S. Madanes, eds., *Notre Amerique Metisse* (Paris: Decouvert, 1992). On the independent churches in Africa, some regard them as Christian, for example, Eboussi Boulaga, *Christianity without Fetishes* (Maryknoll, N.Y.: Orbis

Books, 1984); others appreciate their inculturating meaning, for example, Kossi Tossou, "Chancen und Schwierigkeiten der Inculturation in Afrika," in *Die Theologische-Praktishe Quartalschrift* 1 (1991), pp. 49-57.

6. Aloysius Pieris, "Inter-religious Dialogue and Theology of Religions," *Voices from the Third World* 15/2 (1992), p. 188.

7. See Paulo Suess, "Inculturação," *Revista Eclesiastica Brasileira* 49/193 (1989), pp. 115-117; Teresa Okure, "Inculturation, Biblical and Theological Basis," *Inculturation of Christianity in Africa* (Eldoret: Gaba Publications, 1990), pp. 55-88; Robert Schreiter, "A Framework for a Discussion on Inculturation," in *Mission in Dialogue*, ed. M. Motte and J. Lang (Maryknoll, N.Y.: Orbis Books, 1982), pp. 544-556; Peter Schineller, *A Handbook on Inculturation* (Mahwah N.J.: Paulist, 1990); Antonio do Carmo Cheuiche, *Evangelización de la Cultura e Inculturación del Evangelio* (Bogotá: CELAM, 1988); and signs of Latin American openness toward Asian and African issues in idem, *Evangelización de la Cultura e Inculturación del Evangelio* (Buenos Aires: Guadalupe, 1986).

8. Karl Rahner, *Theological Investigations*, vol. 4 (London: Darton, Longman, Todd, 1966), p. 116.

9. Ibid., p. 109.

10. A. Cheuiche, *Evangelización de la Cultura e Inculturación del Evangelio*, p. 49; B. Carrasco, *Inculturación del Evangelio* (Basílica de Guadalupe, Mexico), no. 42 (May 12, 1993).

11. M. M'nteba, "La inculturación de la tercera iglesia: pentecostés de Dios o desquite de las culturas," *Concilium* 239 (1992), p. 182.

12. José Comblin, "Perspectiva sobre la cultura," in *Teologia y Cultura* (Santiago: Facultad de Teología, 1992), p. 29; cf. idem, *The Holy Spirit and Liberation* (Maryknoll, N.Y.: Orbis Books, 1989).

13. P. Suess, *La Nueva Evangelización* (Quito: Abya Yala, 1991), p. 228.

14. Franz Damen explains it as follows: "Assimilation of the faith from within one's own culture, so that it becomes authentically incarnated (*Hacia una Teología de la Inculturación* [La Paz: CRB, 1989]). For his part, Leonardo Boff stresses that it is a process, a process and an encounter in which "culture assimilates the gospel on the basis of its own cultural matrices" (*Nova Evangelização* [Petrópolis: Vozes, 1990], p. 24).

15. John Paul II, "Speech to the Pontifical Council for Culture," January 18, 1983. On this point a member of that council says: "In the Latin American context the evangelization of culture represents the challenge of creating a new polis of communion and participation" (Pedro Morandé, *Cultura y Evangelizacin en América Latina* [Santiago: Paulinas, 1988], p. 40). For his part, Cardinal Ratzinger says that it is preferable to speak of "interculturality" (rather than *inculturation*) because this latter term "presumes that a culturally naked faith is transplanted to a religiously indifferent culture" (text in *El Mercurio* [October 10, 1993], E:10).

16. This question is raised by Sergio Silva, "Cultura e inculturación en el documento de Santo Domingo," *Medellín* (1993).

3. RENEWAL OF CATECHESIS

1. The culture market has been set up in some nations, such as Brazil, since the 1960s. See R. Ortiz, *A Moderna Tradição Brasileira* (Sao Paulo: Brasiliense, 1988). In some countries there is a great deal of production of foreign things, but the general tendency is toward consolidation of regional markets linked to worldwide

globalization (see J. J. Brunner, *América Latina: Cultura y Modernidad* [Mexico: Grijalbo, 1995]).

2. I here take up some strands of a wide-ranging discussion: Rodolfo Kush, *Pensamiento Indígena y Popular en América Latina* (Buenos Aires: ICA, 1973); Aníbal Quijano, *Modernidad, Identidad y Utopía en América Latina* (Lima: Socialismo y Participación, 1988); Franz Hinkelammert, *Democracia y Totalitarismo* (San José: DEI, 1987) and *Teología del Mercado Total* (La Paz: HISBOL, 1989); D. Sobrevilla and P. Belaunde, *Qué Modernidad Deseamos: el Conflicto entre Nuestra Tradición y lo Nuevo* (Lima: Epígrafe, 1994).

3. J. C. Scannone, *Evangelización, Cultura y Teología* (Buenos Aires: Guadalupe, 1990); P. Morandé, *Cultura y Modernización en América Latina* (Santiago: Universidad Católica, 1984) and *Evangelización de la Cultura y Modernización* (Lima: VE, 1988); J. Comblin, *Reconciliación y Liberación* (Santiago: CESOC, 1987) and *Called for Freedom: The Changing Context of Liberation Theology* (Maryknoll, N.Y.: Orbis Books, 1998), pp. 138-170; J. B. Libanio, "Modernidad y desafíos evangelizadores," in *Vida, Clamor y Esperanza* (Bogotá: Paulinas, 1992).

4. There are some three hundred definitions of culture, according to Kroeber and Kluckholm, *Culture: A Critical Review of Concepts and Definitions* (New York, 1952).

5. M. Dhavamony, S.J., "Problemática actual de la inculturación del Evangelio," in *Evangelización de la Cultura e Inculturación del Evangelio* (Buenos Aires: Guadalupe, 1988), p. 143, and his "The Christian Theology of Inculturation," *Studia Missionalia* 44 (1995), pp. 1-44; J. Sahi "Popular Spirituality in India," *SEDOS* 89/5, p. 151 (he lives with his family in an ashram; he deals with the challenge of inculturation not with regard to the philosophy of an elite but in view of the life and religion of ordinary people in India).

6. International Theological Commission, *Fede e inculturazione* (1988), no. 11, in *Il Regno-Documenti* 9 (1989), p. 275. There are three sections: vision from the standpoint of Christian anthropology (a philosophical option), inculturation in the history of salvation, and contemporary problems (three crucial issues: religiosities, young churches, modernity).

7. Alfredo Morin notes: "Inculturation of the faith culminates in the Incarnation: the Word became Jewish, not to remain that way forever but in order to then quickly become Arab, Cretan, Guaraní, Quechua, Bantu" ("La inculturación de la fe en la Iglesia Apostólica," presentation at the DECAT-CELAM seminar, Bogotá, 1989, p. 2).

8. See P. Suess, *La Nueva Evangeliación* (Quito: Abya Yala, 1991), pp. 183-235; I take up the main lines here.

9. In this regard, see L. Luzbetak, *The Church and Cultures* (Maryknoll, N.Y.: Orbis Books, 1988), p. 69. P. Suess, op. cit., notes that the magisterium takes up the postcolonial spirit which goes beyond "translating" the message into the culture.

10. Further comments can be found in "El Nuevo catecismo ¿animará la policromía católica?," my presentation to the national meeting organized by the Bishops' Commission on Catechesis, Lima, 1993. The Spanish Catechesis Association stresses the value of the 1992 catechism as a reference point and suggests three signs of its inculturation: in ethnic cultures, by ages of those being catechized, and in modern culture ("El catecismo de la Iglesia Católica," *Ecclesia* 2617 [1993], pp. 6-10).

11. I am citing *Lineas Communes de Orientación para la Catequesis en América Latina* (1986) (guidelines decided by two CELAM Assemblies, 1981 and 1983);

and DECAT-CELAM, *Hacia una Catequesis Inculturada*, conference proceedings, II Semana Latinoamericana de Catequesis, Caracas (1994) (the most outstanding presentations are those of R. Viola, W. Gruen, A. Salvatierra, A. Morin, B. Cansi, E. García, A. Calderón, and F. van den Bosch).

12. I am citing *Catechese Renovada* (CNBB do Brasil: Paulinas, 1987), to which people working in catechesis all over the country at all levels made contributions. The major divisions in the text are history of catechesis, principles, fundamental issues, catechizing community. I also cite *En Camino Hacia el Reino de Dios,* sixteen catechetical charts made by people in collaboration with the Department of Catechesis of the Bishops' Conference of Ecuador (1983).

13. In the Chilean case I am examining "Al encuentro del Dios vivo" (parents' books), workbooks for boy or girl, teachers' manuals, celebrations for children, auxiliary texts (by in the late 1980s some four million of these texts had been published); in the text I am citing *Metodología*, Catequesis Familiar (1988), p. 25. In the diocese of Cajamarca (under in the wise leadership of Bishop José Dammert) catechesis of adults uses *Vamos Caminando* (Lima: CEP, 1977), catechesis of children uses *Buscamos el Camino* (Cajamarca/ CEP, 1987), *Celebraciones de la Vida Cristiana* (Cajamarca, 1988), and other texts.

14. See Comisión Episcopal de Evangelización y Catequesis, *Guía Pastoral para la Catequesis de México* (1992), especially 33-61, 66-102; DECAT-CELAM, *Hacia una Catequesis Inculturada,* Conclusiones, 35-68, 87-116.

15. Op. cit. note 5 above.

16. Juan Carlos Scannone, "Pastoral de la cultura hoy en América Latina," in *Evangelización de la Cultura e Inculturación del Evangelio* (Buenos Aires, 1988), p. 263.

4. MISSION IN THE LIFE OF THE PEOPLE

1. The aftermath of Vatican Council II has seen an affirmation of forms of the mission of the laity, the form of mission of members of religious congregations living in the midst of the poor (CLAR *Vida Religiosa en América Latina a partir de Medellín* [Bogotá: CLAR, 1976], pp. 32-35), the local church as missionary (Puebla), and also small communities (SD 48), "initiative and boldness to discover new fields for the evangelizing activity of the Church" (Puebla 806; cf. SD 97), lay people as "active agents of the new evangelization." Missionary congresses in Latin America have outlined the mission within and mission toward other cultures in the world (1977 and 1983 in Mexico, 1987 in Bogotá, 1991 in Lima, 1995 in Belo Horizonte).

2. Two decades ago J. Comblin noted the original meaning of mission in "Actualidad da teologia da missão," *Revista Eclesiastica Brasileira* 32/129 (1972), pp. 796-925, 33/131 (1973), pp. 5-34, 579-603.

3. J. Daniélou, *Le Mystère du Salut des Nations* (Paris: Seuil, 1984). Daniélou warned that unifying Christian civilization was threatened by communist universalism (pp. 13, 19-26). This and other attitudes can be compared with the missionary theology of Vatican II (see J. Lang, "The Specific Missionary Vocation in the Post-Vatican II Period," *Missiology* 16/4 [1988], pp. 387-396).

4. One report on the "Catholic crusade" from the United States toward Latin America sums up its goals as evangelize, promote vocations, and halt the danger from communism (G. Costello, *Mission to Latin America: The Successes and Failures of a Twentieth Century Crusade* [Maryknoll, N.Y.: Orbis Books, 1979], p. 231). Protestant circles speak of campaigns, crusades, and invading Roman territory

(military terminology). This posture began at the Congress of Panama (1916), which is regarded as the "key moment in the cultural expansion of the United States south of the Rio Grande." In the 1960s evangelical sectors had a 10 percent growth rate (R. C. Fernandes, "As missões protestantes en números," *Cadernos do ISER* [Rio de Janeiro] 10, pp. 43-46).

5. See E. Dussel, ed., *Historia General de la Iglesia en América Latina,* eight vols. (Mexico/Salamanca: Paulinas/Sígueme, 1984-1987); P. Suess, ed., *Queimada e Semeadura* (Petrópolis: Vozes, 1988); R. Ballán, *Misioneros de la Primera Hora* (Lima: Misión sin Fronteras, 1991); P. Casaldáliga, "A los 500 años, descolonizar y desevangelizar," *Revista Latinoamericana de Teología* 16 (1989), p. 115. Decolonizing and de-evangelizing mean returning to the sources of Latin American identity and to the sources of Christian faith.

6. Three encyclicals stand out: *Maximum Illud* (1919) of Benedict XV supports the *propaganda fides,* is concerned for the "multitude of souls" sunk in the darkness of death (2) and reminds missionaries to set their gaze on the supernatural "recalling that it is not your calling to expand the frontiers of human empires but those of Christ" (7). Pius XII's *Evangelii Praecones* (1951) reaffirms the missionary work motivated by the existence of millions of infidels, atheistic materialism, communism, and the non-Catholics in Latin America. Pius XII's *Fidei Donum* (1957) is focused on Africa but also on the expansion of the church in the world (2) and, among other things, on the building of a Christian social order (9). There is thus an evolution from an accent on saving souls to a mission in the world order.

7. Position papers and lines of consensus at SEDOS are found in M. Motte and J. Lang, eds., *Mission in Dialogue* (Maryknoll, N.Y.: Orbis Books, 1982). Those four major directions show that questions in the 1970s of why and how to engage in mission have been well answered.

8. Documents of Melgar and Manaus are found in *Iglesia, Pueblos, y Culturas* 1 (Quito, 1981). The participants at Melgar asked themselves a crucial question: What is the need for and meaning of missionary activity? They replied out of the history of universal salvation. Manaus has traced out the "incarnationist liberating" line (now called the "inculturated liberating" line).

9. Presentations and agreements at COMLA-4 are found in *Memorias del COMLA-4* (Lima: Paulinas/Salesiana, 1991).

10. Works that have taken a fresh look at mission include J. Gorski, *Situaciones Históricas como Contenido del Mensaje Evangélico* (Bogotá: Paulinas, 1975); the collective work *Antropología y Teología Misionera* (Bogotá: Paulinas, 1975), which includes a Trinitarian reflection by C. Siller; S. Galilea, *Responsabilidad Misionera de América Latina* (México: Misiones Culturales, 1981); C. Pape, et al., *La Misión desde América Latina* (Bogotá: CLAR, 1982); the collective work *A Missão a partir de América Latina* (Sao Paulo: Paulinas, 1983); J. Gorski, *El Desarrollo Histórico de la Misionología en América Latina* (La Paz, 1985); O. Osorio, *Lo Misional Hoy a partir de América Latina* (Bogotá: CELAM-DEMIS, 1987); R. Aubry, *El Compromiso Misionero de América Latina* (Lima: Obras Misionales, 1989); E. Gartolucci, *La Misión desde la Pobreza* (Lima: Obras Misionales, 1989); the collective work *Práticas Misionarias Latinoamericanas* (Sao Paulo: Sem Fronteras, 1990); M. Pozo, *Vayan y Anuncien la Fe* ((Lima: Paulinas, 1990); R. Auri, *La Misión Siguiendo a Jesús por los Caminos de América Latina* (Buenos Aires: Guadalupe, 1990); R. Ballán, *El Valor de Salir, la Apertura de América Latina a la Misión Universal* (Lima: Paulinas, 1990), which emphasizes the option for the poor and

Marian devotion, pp. 163-181; L. A. Castro, *Espiritualidad Misionera* (Bogotá: Paulinas, 1991); A. Antoniazzi and C. Caliman, eds., *A Presença da Igreja na Cidade* (Petrópolis: Vozes, 1994).

11. L. Boff, *Trinity and Society* (Maryknoll, N.Y.: Orbis Books, 1988).

12. Interview with G. Gutiérrez in *Misión sin Fronteras* (Lima) 129 (1991), pp. 20-25.

13. Aubry, *El Compromiso*, p. 17. Aubry goes on to say that the commitment of the poor to the poor is what "opens the doors to peoples and cultures" (p. 21). This runs against the common opinion that missionary successes is due to works that attract multitudes of beneficiaries; rather the key to success is the ability of God's poor people.

14. As J. Smutko puts it, this "exodus" shows the failure of Catholic mission to inculturate ("La actividad de la Iglesia," *Senderos* 37 [1990], p. 68).

15. P. Suess, "Culturas indígenas y evangelización," in *Iglesia, Pueblos, y Culturas* 3 (1986), p. 31 (a talk given in 1980). As Suess notes, some church circles are sensitive to the poor, but they do not have this same openness "when it comes to the other, to the ethnically and religiously different" (*Iglesia, Pueblos, y Culturas* 4 [1987], 111). Also see Suess, *Evangelizar a partir dos Projetos Historicos dos outros: Ensaio de Missiologia* (Sao Paulo: Paulus, 1995).

16. D. J. Bosch, *Transforming Mission: Paradigm Shifts in Theology of Mission* (Maryknoll, N.Y.: Orbis Books, 1996), pp. 455-456.

17. Aubry, *El Compromiso*, p. 14.

18. Here is a clear stance: "The problem of the syncretism of many believers must be faced with love, understanding, competence, creativity and patience; otherwise our believing people would be exposed to continual manipulation" (Conclusions of the Second Latin American Week of Catechesis, *Hacia una Catequesis Inculturada* [Bogotá: CELAM, 1995], 79 [p. 381]; cf. 177 [p. 403]).

5. RELIGION OF THE POOR

1. X. Gorostiaga, "La mediación de las ciencias sociales y los cambios internacionales," in *Cambio Social y Pensamiento Cristiano en América Latina* (Madrid: Trotta, 1993), p. 131 (this work includes a specifically Latin American agenda). Cf. a moderate proposal in *Neoliberales y Pobres* (Bogotá: CINEP, 1993), pp. 529-542.

2. M. Marzal, "Syncretismo iberoamericano e inculturación," mimeo (1989), p. 1. Marzal also notes that it is a resistance of Indians and blacks to Christianization (cf. his "Análisis teológico-pastoral del sincretismo," *Antigua* 26 [1985], pp. 69-86, and *El Sincretismo Iberoamericano* [Lima: PUC, 1985]). For his part, J. Ansión, *Desde el Rincón de los Muertos* (Lima: Gredes, 1987), p. 52, explains that in the conflict between social and cultural worlds syncretism is sometimes resistance and on other occasions is a tool of control.

3. See, for example, an adaptation of a Roman and European form in Congregación para el Culto, "La liturgia romana y la inculturacion," *L'Osservatore Romano* (April 8, 1994), pp. 5-10. In view of this, J. Yañez, SDB (*Servicio* 186 [1994], p. 26) points out that the most accessible path—popular religion—is thereby closed to a possible inculturation.

4. From a proposal of Christan culture in the singular, see SD 22, 24, 31, 33, 45, 97, 229; some are going on to formulate it in the plural.

5. In this regard, see chapter 1 of this work.

6. P. Suess, "A historia dos outros escrita por nos," *Evangelizar a partir dos Projetos Historicos dos outros* (Sao Paulo: Paulus, 1995), pp. 61-90; G. Gutiérrez, *La Fuerza Histórica de los Pobres* (Lima: CEP, 1979), p. 370 (in English, *The Power of the Poor in History* [Maryknoll, N.Y.: Orbis Books, 1983]).

7. Solange Alberro, "Acerca de la primera evangelización en México," in *La Venida del Reino*, ed. G. Ramos (Cusco: Las Casas, 1994), p. 25.

8. Fray Diego Durán, *Ritos y Fiestas de los Antiguos Mexicanos (1576-1578)* (Mexico: Innovación, 1980), chap. 84, p. 118.

9. See details on Brazil in O. Beozzo, "Irmandades, santuarios e capelinhas de beira da estrada," *Revista Eclesiástica Brasileira* 148 (1977), pp. 741-748; R. Azzi, *O Catholicismo Popular no Brasil* (Petrópolis: Vozes, 1978). For a case in Mexico, see I. Castillo, *San Pueblo* (Mexico: CRT, 1979), pp. 33-35.

10. E. Lopez, *500 Años de Resistencia y de Lucha de los Pueblos de América contra la Opresión*, mimeo (Chiapas, 1991), p. 18.

11. C. Duverger, *La Conversión de los Indios de la Nueva España* (Quito: Abya Yala, 1990), pp. 238-244; Duverger even talks about a "Christian practice of idolatry" (p. 244). I offer a vision of syncretism "from below" in my book *Cultura y Fe Latinoamericana* (Santiago: Rehue, 1994), chap. 7.

12. I am using J. P. Viqueira, "La ilustración y las fiestas religiosas populares en la ciudad de México 1730-1821," *Cuicuilco* 14/15 (1984), pp. 7-14; and data on the most important colonial synod in Chile, *Sínodos de Santiago de Chile 1688 y 1763* (Madrid, Salamanca: CISC, 1983), pp. 337-339, 340-343.

13. *Sínodos de Santiago*, chap. 12, p. 204.

14. In this regard see J. Barnadas, *La Iglesia Católica en Bolivia* (La Paz: Juventud, 1976), p. 47; J. Pinto "Etnocentrismo y etnocidio," in *Sentido Histórico del V Centenario*, ed. G. Meléndez (San José: DEI, 1992), p. 122.

15. See my chapter on celebrations in *Catolicism Popular* (Petrópolis: Vozes, 1993), pp. 131-159.

16. One can draw out the inculturations in each world of celebration. For the Mayan and Tarahumara worlds, see E. Vogt, *Ofrendas para los Dioses* (Mexico: FCE, 1983); W. Smith, *El Sistema de Fiestas y el Cambio Económico* (Mexico: FCE, 1981); P. de Velasco, *Danzar o Morir* (Mexico CRT, 1987). For urban settings, see V.A. Campana, *Fiesta y Poder* (Quito: Abya Yala, 1991); X. Albó and M. Preiswerk, *Los Señores del Gran Poder* (La Paz: CTP, 1986); C. Rodriguez B., *Sacerdotes de Viola* (Petrópolis: Vozes, 1981).

17. For overviews of Marian feasts, see R. Vargas U., *Historia del Culto de María en Iberoamérica* (Buenos Aires: Huarpes, 1947); collective work, *Nuestra Señora de América* (Bogotá: CELAM, 1988).

18. J. Klaiber, *Religión y Revolución en el Perú, 1824-1976* (Lima: Universidad del Pacífico, 1980), p. 42.

19. I. Vega C., "Sistemas de creencias," *Nueva Sociedad* 136 (1995), p. 60.

20. H. de Lima Vaz, in *O Impacto da Modernidade sobre a Religião*, ed. M. C. Bingemer (Sao Paulo: Loyola, 1992), p. 121.

21. Vega C., art cit., p. 60.

22. P. Suess, ed., *A Conquista da América Espanhola* (Petrópolis: Vozes, 1992) cites texts of the Third Council of Lima and Third Council of Mexico (pp. 368 and 394); C. Duverger, op. cit., pp. 93-94, 98-100 (discussion of the twelve Franciscans). For reform in modernity, see Concilio Plenario de América Latina, *Actas y Decretos* (Rome, 1899), chap. 6, para. 159; and, in Brazil, P. Ribeiro de O., *Religião e*

Dominação de Clase (Petrópolis: Vozes, 1985), who quotes from the 1915 document (pp. 290 and 298).

23. P. Berger, *Para una Teoría Sociológica de la Religión* (Barcelona: Kairós, 1981), p.176.

24. See the case studies in D. Martin, *Tongues of Fire* (Oxford: Basil Blackwell, 1990), pp. 165-171; F. C. Rolim, *Pentecostalismo: Brasil e América Latina* (Petrópolis: Vozes, 1994); W. Kapsoli, *Guerreros de la Oración* (Lima: SEPEC, 1994).

25. Ribeiro, op cit., pp. 310-311.

26. J. C. Cortázar, *Secularización, Cambio y Continuidad en el Catholicismo Peruano* (Lima: PUC and BDLC, 1997), pp. 63-88.

27. F. Hinkelammert, *Theology of the Total Market* (La Paz: HISBOL, 1989), p. 59.

28. W. Beinert, "Historia e historicidad," *Diccionario de Teología Dogmática* (Barcelona: Herder, 1990), p. 328.

29. C. Parker, *Otra Lógica en América Latina: Religión Popular y Modernización Capitalista* (Santiago/Mexico: FCE, 1993), pp. 153-202, 323-346.

30. I cite proposals from Bishop Javier Lozano, "Reflexiones para la inculturación de Catecismo," in *Hacia una Catequesis Inculturada* (Bogota: CELAM, 1995), pp. 81-82; Bishops' Conference of Bolivia, *Directrices Pastorales 1994-98* (La Paz, 1994); objective 2, A. A. Antoniazzi, "A inculturação da fe cristã no Brasil de hoje," in *Desafios da Missão* (Sao Paulo: Mundo e Missão, 1995), pp. 111-113.

31. Suess, *Evangelizar a partir dos Projetos Historicos dos outros*, 1995.

32. Sor Juana Inés de la Cruz, *Obras Completas* (Mexico: Porrúa, 1996), p. 865.

33. The issue of inculturation that is plural in nature is raised from many angles. See an excellent example in the work of the Society for Theology and the Study of Religion in Brazil, *Inculturação, Desafios de Hoje* (Petrópolis: Vozes, 1994), in which P. Suess discusses inculturation from the indigenous angle, Da Silva as an Afro-American, H. Assman as a social scientist, Jung Mo Sung in political terms, P. Guareschi in the area of communications, and Dom M. P. Caravalheira as a pastor. Inculturation obviously cannot be enclosed within the religious and cultural spheres.

6. ANDEAN RELIGIOUS LIFE

1. Servio Silva, Joao B. Libanio, and Victor Codina provide positive clues in this direction in their articles "¿Puede enriquecerse la vida religiosa con la cultura moderna?," "Dimensión profética de la vida religiosa en la sociedad moderna," and "Modernidad y consejos evangélicos," all in *Testimonio* 157 (1996), pp. 29-34, 35-42, 43-48. On the underlying issues, see H. Urbano, ed., *Tradición y Modernidad en los Andes* (Cusco: Las Casas, 1992); D. Sobrevilla and P. Belaúnde, eds., *¿Qué Modernidad Deseamos?* (Lima: Epígrafe, 1994); J. Larraín, *Modernidad, Razón e Identidad en América Latina* (Santiago: Andrés Bello, 1996).

2. I incorporate here portions of an earlier work, "Identidades emergentes y carismas religiosos," *Inculturación* 1/2 (1995), pp. 33-44.

3. I recommend Paulo Suess, "La disputa por la inculturación," *Evangelizar desde los Proyectos Históricos de los Otros* (Quito: Abya Yala, 1995), pp. 187-207; *Evangelización de la Cultura e Inculturación del Evangelio* (Buenos Aires: Guadalupe, 1988); *Inculturazione* (Roma: Centrum Ignatianum Spiritualitatis, 1990); Marcio F. dos Ajos, ed., *Inculturação: Desafios de Hoje* (Petrópolis: Vozes, 1994); M. F. dos Anjos, ed., *Teologia da Inculturação e Inculturação da Teologia* (Petrópolis: Vozes and SOTER, 1995); Simón Pedro Arnold, *La Otra Orilla: Una Espiritualidad de la Inculturación* (Lima: CEP, 1996).

4. CLAR (Latin American Confederation of Religious), *Tendencias Proféticas de la Vida Religiosa en América Latina*, doc. 24 (Bogotá: CLAR, 1975), p. 69; see also Libanio, art. cit.

5. V. Codina, "Vida religiosa y evangelizacion en América Latina," *Boletín de la CLAR*, 27/1-2 (1989), pp. 21, 25 (in this text inculturation receives only a brief mention on p. 26); see his work on inculturation, *Creo en el Espíritu Santo* (Santander: Sal Terrae, 1994), pp. 189-214.

6. In 1 Cor 12:4-11: wisdom, knowledge, faith, healing, miracles, prophecy, discernment of spirits, tongues and its interpretation. In Rom 12:6-8: prophecy, ministry, teaching, exhortation, giving, presiding, showing mercy. In Eph 4: 7-12: being an apostle, a prophet, evangelizer, pastor, teacher. These lists, besides showing the multiple forms and orders of charisms, also serve to inspire all of human existence (and are not limited to "the religious").

7. On a continent-wide level CLAR for a time stressed the spirituality of sharing life with the poor and solidarity; see, for example, *La Vida según el Espíritu*, doc. 14 (Bogotá: CLAR, 1974); C. Maccise, *Nueva Espiritualidad de la Vida Religiosa en América Latina*, doc. 30 (Bogotá: CLAR, 1977). In the 1990s (after Santo Domingo) inculturation began to be discussed; see F. Taborda, *Evangelización para el Tercer Milenio*, doc. 65 (Bogotá: CLAR, 1994), pp. 143-146; 150-152, and the objectives and inspiring lines passed by CLAR General Assemblies in 1994 and 1997.

8. N. Zevallos and V. Codina, *Vida Religiosa: Historia y Teología* (Madrid: Paulinas, 1987), pp. 106-108.

9. Cf. John Paul II, *Vita Consecrata* (1996), 79 and 80.

10. See Compañía de Jesús, "Nuestra misión y la cultura," 34a. Congregación General (1995); Pasionistas, *La Inculturación del Carisma Pasionista y la Modernidad* (Lima, 1996) and J. A. Orbegozo, Superior General, *La Vida Consagrada Puede Ofrecer una Aportación Original a los Retos de la Inculturación* (Rome, 1997).

11. C. Maccise, *Nueva Espiritualidad de la Vida Religiosa en América Latina* (Bogotá: CLAR, 1977), p. 26.

7. Catholic Identity and the Good News Today

1. Bishops of the Southern Andes of Peru, pastoral letter, *Impulsados por el Espíritu* (1995), no. 21.

2. C. Parker, *Popular Religion and Modernization in Latin America: A Different Logic* (Maryknoll, N.Y.: Orbis Books, 1996), pp. 239ff.

3. See Xavier Gorostiaga, "Ciudadanos del planeta y del siglo XXI," *Envío* (Universidad Centroamericana) 157 (1995); R. Ortiz, *Mundialização e Cultura* (Sao Paulo: Brasiliense, 1994), pp. 171-185; and "Consejo para un Parlamento de Religiones del Mundo," *Hacia una Ética Global* (1993).

4. For an overview, see my chapter "Celebrations of Catholic Faith," in *Catolicismo Popular* (Petrópolis: Vozes, 1993), pp. 131-159.

5. Document of the 34th General Congregation of the Society of Jesus (1995), section 1.1.3, no. 17.

6. Antonio M. Kater Filho has systematized what he does in "Anunciamos a Jesús," a program on a national television channel, and has published *Marketing Applied to the Catholic Church* (Sao Paulo: Loyola, 1994), a text that I cite extensively without placing quotation marks. In the U.S. context, see J. Considine,

Marketing Your Church: Concepts and Strategies (New York: Sheed and Ward, 1996); G. Barna, *Marketing the Church* (Colorado: Navpress, 1988); R. L. Moore, *Selling God: American Religion in the Market Place of Culture* (New York: Oxford, 1994).

7. Interview with Fr. Leo T. Pereira in a special report on the Charismatic Renewal in Brazil, *Veja* 141 (1995), p. 73.

8. *Taller de Teología Aymara* 1990, publication of the Instituto de Estudios Aymaras, Peru (1991).

9. Victor Codina, "A fe do povo pobre," *Perspectiva Teológica* 27 (1995), p. 184.

10. Conferencia Episcopal Peruana, *Reflexiones y Lineas Pastorales para el período 1995-2000* (Lima, 1995). A number of commentaries on Santo Domingo place all the emphasis on Christian culture and give practically no importance to inculturation (see, for example, Javier García, *Nueva Evangelización y Cultura Cristiana en el Documento de Santo Domingo* [Lima: Vida y Espiritualidad, 1993], pp. 39-64).

11. The texts of Commission No. 26 of the Fourth conference, in their fourth and final version (approved unanimously on November 21, 1992, but modified by the Central Drafting Commission). I am using the collection prepared by Paulo Suess (who has made fundamental contributions before and during Santo Domingo). I cite the last two paragraphs of Commission No. 26 (suppressed by the Central Drafting Commission), which clearly propose an inculturated church.

Index